Exploring the Myths and Realities of Today's Schools

A Candid Review of the Challenges Educators Face

Richard P. McAdams

ROWMAN & LITTLEFIELD EDUCATION
A division of
ROWMAN & LITTLEFIELD PUBLISHERS, INC.
Lanham • *New York* • *Toronto* • *Plymouth, UK*

Published by Rowman & Littlefield Education
A division of Rowman & Littlefield Publishers, Inc.
A wholly owned subsidary of The Rowman & Littlefield Publishing Group, Inc.
4501 Forbes Boulevard, Suite 200, Lanham, Maryland 20706
http://www.rowmaneducation.com

Estover Road, Plymouth PL6 7PY, United Kingdom

British Library Cataloguing in Publication Information Available

Library of Congress Cataloging-in-Publication Data
McAdams, Richard P.
   Exploring the myths and realities of today's schools : a candid review of the challenges educators face / Richard P. McAdams.
      p. cm.
   Includes bibliographical references.
   ISBN 978-1-60709-849-2 (cloth : alk. paper) — ISBN 978-1-60709-850-8 (pbk. : alk. paper) — ISBN 978-1-60709-851-5 (electronic)
   1. Public schools—United States. I. Title.
   LA217.2M391 2010
   370.973—dc22   2010018494

♾ ™ The paper used in this publication meets the minimum requirements of American National Standard for Information Sciences—Permanence of Paper for Printed Library Materials, ANSI/NISO Z39.48-1992.

Printed in the United States of America

To the thousands of caring, competent, and conscientious educators who have inspired me during my forty-five years in public education.

Contents

List of Tables

Preface

What is the real status of public education in the United States? Are the critics right when they say that our schools are failing? Or perhaps the educational pundits in the academy and the media are missing some positive data while overgeneralizing from negative stereotypes that inform conventional wisdom. Today more than fifty million children attend our public schools, representing approximately 87 percent of all school-age children.

The proportion of students attending public schools has changed little over past decades, and the proportions are unlikely to change in the future. When I began teaching in 1965 there were many impassioned critiques of American public education, such as Rudolf Flesch's *Why Johnny Can't Read* and Hyman Rickover's *Swiss Schools and Ours: Why Theirs Are Better*.

Forty-five years later we are still treated to polemical books with the same message about the failure of our public schools. Two current representative titles include *The Nightmare That Is Public Education* by Renato C. Nicolai and *Dumbing Us Down* by John Taylor Gatto. This book genre usually offers questionable solutions to the perceived problems that strike the experienced public school educator as naïve and overblown, if not wrongheaded.

The problems cited and the policy prescriptions offered exhibit an uncanny familiarity over this entire period. Why have we not had significant improvements in our educational system over these forty-plus years and why do the prescriptions for improvement either fail to be implemented or fail in practice?

Yes, there have been gains here and there and now and then, but few significant systemic improvements have occurred. From Marva Collins's success with inner-city Chicago children in the 1980s through the achievements of the Kipp Charter Schools and the Harlem Children's Zone in recent years, we have seen flashes of real progress, but such progress thus far has been either unsustainable or not transferable to the wider public school system.

During my long career I've witnessed several broad trends in education. In 1965 the schools were still attempting to attain greater academic rigor following the Sputnik launching by the Soviet Union in the late 1950s. This was before the age of student revolts and court-mandated expansion of student rights that led to a more lax school environment in the 1970s. In my opinion, schools reached their nadir of effectiveness in the mid-1970s.

With the *A Nation at Risk* report in 1983, schools began to shed the worst elements of the freewheeling 1970s, and greater academic rigor became a higher priority. This push for academic excellence has continued to the present with some successes. The little-discussed reality, however, is that the nature of the student body has changed significantly since the 1960s, with today's teachers challenged by a far higher proportion of students from socially and economically disadvantaged backgrounds.

In the early 1990s public education witnessed a rising enthusiasm for charter schools and voucher programs. These initiatives have shown some signs of success, but their influence has been minimal after almost twenty years. Why is this? For more than two decades we have experienced numerous state and federal initiatives designed to dramatically improve student achievement. Here, too, the results have been meager.

This book is neither a polemic nor an exposé. While it is certainly not a memoir, I do offer some illustrative vignettes from my years in the public schools as a teacher, principal, and superintendent. Drawing on my forty-plus years of experience in the schools, I critique the myriad prescriptions for school reform and identify those recommendations that are on target, partially on target, or totally wrongheaded.

In addition to personal experiences in the schools, I have also benefited from six years serving as executive director of the School Study Council at Lehigh University. This group of more than forty superintendents met five or six times each year to discuss issues of current interest and concern. This experience provided me with valuable insight into the workings of forty school districts over a long time period.

My years teaching at Lehigh also allowed me to interact in classes with hundreds of aspiring and practicing school administrators. These "teachable moments" also gave me a broader perspective for interpreting my own experiences in the schools. My consulting work and supervision of administrative interns provided many additional opportunities to visit schools and interact with educators from every type of school district.

Much that is written about the public schools is from the theoretical perspective of college professors, think tank experts, or media pundits. This viewpoint often paints public education with too broad a brush to be helpful. Others write from the more personal perspective of a classroom teacher or perhaps a school principal. This perspective often provides too narrow or idiosyncratic a view. My hope is that my conclusions will be narrow enough to connect with the reality in the schools yet broad enough to be useful in the national conversation about improving public education.

My review examines the major factors identified by critics as inimical to good performance and analyzes the practicality of the major recommendations for improvement by these critics. The most common criticisms of the schools include the deleterious effects of teachers unions, an inequitable finance system, the poor quality of teachers, and cumbersome school bureaucracies. I also explore several other salient features of schools that are seldom discussed but have an impact on school quality.

Proposed solutions by public school critics include merit pay for teachers, charter schools and vouchers to promote competition, increasing the length of the school year and school day, closer supervision and evaluation of teachers, and tougher controls over teachers unions through legislation.

I explore several additional issues that are seldom addressed. These include the limits of local control of schools, the corrosive effect of excessive teacher workloads, the negative impact of unreasonable or indifferent parents, and the negative influence on student achievement by a growing number of disadvantaged students. I also explain the nature of schools as organizations and how the prevailing organizational structure inevitably interferes with large-scale reform plans.

Providing a context for the discussion is critically important. Several elements of this context include international comparisons of student achievement, the changing demographics of the schools, and the increasing legal constraints facing public school teachers and administrators. Seventeen years ago I authored a book comparing American public education with that in five other first-world countries (Canada, Germany, England, Denmark, and Japan).

I found much to admire in these other countries, while making many recommendations for improving our schools. I came away with a great pride and respect for what we are achieving in our schools, despite the significant gap between our highest hopes and the current reality.

My major conclusion is that we can and should do more to make our good public school system better. The good news is that in some respects our schools can improve dramatically with relatively minor changes and at a modest cost. The major challenge is that the best solutions call for some politically difficult changes in our approach to schooling.

Readers should keep in mind that many of the judgments in the book are based upon the relatively broad experiences of one individual, many but not all of which can be supported by research. It is obviously impossible for any individual to fully capture the practices and activities of one hundred thousand schools across a broadly diverse nation. Nonetheless, I believe that the opinions and judgments expressed in the book are broadly reflective of reality in America's public schools.

My targeted audiences for the book are parents of school-age children as well as members of the general public with an interest in public education. Practicing teachers and administrators will find much that is familiar to them while gaining a fuller understanding of how the parts of the system interact in real life.

A full appreciation of the breadth and depth of the challenges facing our educators will make us more appreciative of what has been achieved by our public schools. Such an appreciation will also make us more supportive of the constructive changes needed to better serve our students and country through our public schools.

Acknowledgments

A special thank-you to all of my former colleagues who generously gave of their time to read an early version of the manuscript. Their insights and perspectives were a major contribution to the final manuscript. Linda Grobman and Bruce Sensenig offered an "in-the-trenches" perspective of practicing school superintendents. John DeFlaminis provided valuable insights as both a former superintendent and the current executive director of the Penn Center for Educational Leadership at the University of Pennsylvania.

George White, professor of educational leadership at Lehigh University, offered his perspective based on more than twenty-five years of teaching, research, and consulting in the area of school leadership. Harris Sokoloff, director of the Center for School Study Councils at the University of Pennsylvania, provided insights based on almost thirty years of interactions with hundreds of school superintendents through his work with the study council.

I am especially indebted to of my former school board presidents at three different school districts. John Hagen, Kathy Fisher, and Cindy Quinn inspired me with their enthusiasm, commitment, and insight as we jointly met the challenges of school governance during the time we worked together. They each offered insightful commentary on the manuscript, particularly the sections of the book dealing with school governance issues.

I offer my appreciation to Sandy Mangano and Andrea Chipego, two experienced high-level school leaders who were particularly helpful in their areas of special expertise—curriculum and special education. Special thanks also to my wife, Pat, who edited the original manuscript and offered valuable suggestions on many elements of the book.

1

Teachers—The Heart of the Matter

"A teacher affects eternity; he can never tell where his influence stops."

Henry Adams

In the strictest sense education is about the relationship between the teacher and the student. We all can reflect on teachers in our lives who have helped shape our best qualities. They sensed our potential and talents and tried tirelessly to encourage and direct us toward our highest possibilities. Formal instruction was important, but the lessons we learned about character, integrity, and responsibility formed their greatest legacy to us.

This book encompasses all aspects of the world of public education. We will see that much that we think we know is misguided and much of the criticism of our schools and teachers is misplaced. Millions of teachers labor each day to educate their students one child at a time. The conditions in which they labor are far from ideal and the criticisms they endure are largely unwarranted. Consideration of the varied aspects of our public schools will lead us to a better appreciation of the role of our teachers—the heart of the matter.

In responding to the major criticisms of teachers and schools, we of necessity address the issues in the context of the premises and worldview of the principal critics. Most critiques approach schooling from a deficit model. The primary thrust of this model is that the weaknesses in our schools are a question of teacher quality. Teachers are not smart enough, well-educated enough, committed enough, or hard-working enough to properly educate our children. All of these allegations are false, but they need to be refuted. From the perspective of the teacher, the constant stream of criticism reminds them of that parody of management technique that asserts "the beatings will continue until morale improves."

We begin with the issue of teacher quality. When we speak of teacher quality, we immediately think of academic preparation, instructional skill, and basic intelligence. These are the issues addressed in this chapter. There is a much more fundamental and important dimension to the quality question, however, that should be addressed first. This critical dimension concerns the quality of teachers as human beings. What are the virtues of character and personality that the typical teacher brings to his or her work and how do these qualities address the most basic needs of our children?

Educators share the same frailties as the rest of humankind and from time to time a few of them commit spectacularly evil and stupid deeds. Those few educators who sexually exploit children or steal from their schools, for example, receive great notoriety in the local press, and in extreme cases become national pariahs. Similar activities by employees in the private sector, on the other hand, seldom suffer from the same public exposure.

This double standard occurs because we rightly hold those who teach our children to a higher standard. The good news is that 99 percent of educators are worthy of this trust. In a national public school teaching force of 3.2 million, however, that still leaves more than thirty thousand school employees who lack the character necessary to be entrusted with the care of our children.

The great majority of educators are conscientious, dedicated to children, and skilled in their work. They have the qualities of heart and personality necessary to work effectively with young people. For most youngsters in our society, teachers are the principal contact that they have with adults outside the home. Children generally spend about one thousand hours per year with public school teachers over a thirteen-year period between kindergarten and twelfth grade.

Are there some teachers who are not performing conscientiously and competently? Of course there are. The number of such cases, however, is no greater than in other occupations or professions. In fact, the proportion of underperformers may actually be less than in other sectors of our economy and community.

More should be done to remove poor performers from the education profession, as should also be done in other occupations. Our recent national experience with the "masters of the universe" who control Wall Street, the banks, and our automobile companies demonstrates clearly that there is plenty of incompetence in all fields.

The quality of the teaching corps is not a major problem. This is not to say that improvements are not warranted. We don't need to replace large numbers of current teachers or necessarily recruit a higher caliber of teacher in terms of academic ability or preparation. The one caveat is in certain subject areas such as math and the sciences. There is a serious shortage nationally of even minimally certified teachers, much less highly qualified teachers in these subject areas.

Let us turn now to the long-standing and persistent criticism of public school teachers that is ubiquitous in the media and among our cultural and academic elites. The major complaints are that our teachers are not selected from among the top students in our colleges either by academic performance or by ability. Critics cite the comparatively low Scholastic Aptitude Test (SAT) scores of teachers and a lack of academic rigor in colleges of education. They employ the old "those who can do and those who can't teach" mantra to denigrate the competency level of the typical teacher.

Teachers are also commonly criticized for having a shorter workday and shorter work year relative to the general population. The implication is that teaching in general is a relatively easy occupation. Another common criticism is that teachers unions, by stifling any potential progress, control the schools. School administrators also garner much criticism with the charge that they represent an overblown and incompetent bureaucracy.

Let us first address the SAT and academic preparation issues. For generations, teachers have been largely recruited from the lower one-third of college students in terms of the SAT scores of entering college freshmen. This situation is problematic for teachers of math, science, foreign languages, and English. It is less significant for teachers in areas such as physical education, art, and elementary education.

The lower SAT scores in the past have been concentrated among elementary teachers and physical education teachers. Teachers in these areas represent a significant proportion of our teaching corps. Teachers preparing to teach mathematics and the sciences in the period 1994–1997 achieved higher SAT scores on average than did other college graduates (National Science Board, 2004, 26).

The SAT scores for elementary teachers are less critical to student achievement than are the scores of secondary teachers of academic subjects. The level of academic ability needed to teach basic skills at an elementary level is certainly present in the overwhelming majority of our elementary school teachers. Raising the SAT scores, IQ levels, or academic achievement of our elementary school teachers would not materially impact the performance of students. There are several other strategies to improve the educational experience of young students that would have a far greater positive effect.

Academic skill is only one among many factors affecting teacher quality: "Research does suggest that the following factors are associated with teacher quality: having strong academic skills, having appropriate formal training in the field in which they teach and having more than a few years of experience" (National Science Board, 2004, 24).

For those who insist that SAT scores are relevant to teaching effectiveness, there has been some positive news in recent years. The Educational Testing Service (ETS), as noted in a *New York Times* article on December 12, 2007, reported "that teachers who took state licensing exams from 2002 to 2005 scored higher on SATs in high school and earned higher grades in college than their counterparts who took the exams in the mid-1990s" (Dillon, 2007).

Drew H. Gitomer, who conducted the ETS study, claimed, "We're seeing a pretty big jump in qualifications" (Dillon, 2007). The study compared the scores and grade point averages of 153,000 aspiring teachers from twenty states who took the licensing exams from 2002 to 2005, with profiles from 140,000 teachers from the same states from 1994 to 1997. Average SAT scores of teachers in the traditional academic areas were higher than the average SAT scores for the total population of test takers.

SAT scores for elementary school teachers and teachers in most nonacademic areas were lower than the average of all SAT test takers. The fact that the majority of teachers are elementary teachers of grades K–6 depresses the overall SAT average of teachers relative to all SAT takers. It is worth repeating that SAT scores of secondary school academic subject teachers are actually higher than the overall average of all SAT takers.

Ironically, the emphasis on teacher academic ability as it relates to student performance may be highlighted merely because it is easier to quantify than other factors relating to effective teaching. A recent study makes this point by stating that "although traits not measured on standardized tests (such as interpersonal skills, public speaking skills and enthusiasm for working with children) influence whether someone will be an effective teacher, these traits tend to be hard to quantify, and most studies examining the link between teacher skills and student learning limit their definitions of teacher skills to academic skills" (National Science Board, 2002, 35).

The relationship between teacher academic preparation and effectiveness as a teacher has inspired many dissertations. One such dissertation explored the relationship between teachers' undergraduate grade point average, courses in the teachers' certification areas, and teacher effectiveness as evaluated by their building principal. High school teachers of academic subjects were chosen because the relationship between teacher preparation and effectiveness was strongest among these teachers.

The study analyzed the college transcripts of all the academic subject teachers in these high schools. The name of each teacher was placed on an index card. The researcher then met with each high school principal and presented him or her with a stack of index cards with the name of one teacher on each card. Each principal was asked to divide the cards into five stacks, or quintiles, based on his or her judgment, by placing the cards for the most effective teachers in the first quintile and the cards for the least effective teachers in the fifth quintile.

In every case the principals had no trouble identifying teachers for the most-effective quintile and for the least-effective quintile. They found it much more difficult to rate the teachers in the second, third, and fourth quintiles. This result may seem surprising to those who have not been high school principals. High school principals in schools of one to two thousand students, with 60 to 120 teachers, simply did not have the time to concentrate their efforts on teacher effectiveness, except in the more critical cases.

The statistical analyses performed on the relationships between teachers in the top and bottom quintiles and the college transcripts of these two groups produced few positive relationships between grade point average, number of courses taken within the teaching field, and teacher effectiveness as rated by the high school principal. This dissertation indicates that effective teaching is a much more complex variable than can be captured by simply looking at the academic preparation of the teacher (McAdams, 1972).

Effective teaching, as all educators would agree, is actually a very complex art. It can never be captured statistically. The following humorous Internet lore, a whimsical job description for a teacher, makes this point in a somewhat lighthearted manner. While the vignette employs hyperbole to make its point, there is nonetheless much truth in the sentiments expressed.

After being interviewed by the school administration, the teaching prospect said, "Let me see if I've got this right:

- "You want me to go into that room with all those kids, correct their disruptive behavior, observe them for signs of abuse, monitor their dress habits, censor their T-shirt messages, and instill in them a love for learning.
- "You want me to check their backpacks for weapons, wage war on drugs and sexually transmitted diseases, and raise their sense of self-esteem and personal pride.
- "You want me to teach them patriotism and good citizenship; sportsmanship and fair play; and how to register to vote, balance a checkbook, and apply for a job.
- "You want me to check their heads for lice, recognize signs of antisocial behavior, and make sure that they all pass the state exams.
- "You want me to provide them with an equal education regardless of their handicaps, and communicate regularly with their parents by letter, telephone, newsletter, and report card.
- "You want me to do all this with a piece of chalk, a blackboard, a bulletin board, a few books, a big smile, and a starting salary that qualifies me for food stamps.

"You want me to do all this and then you tell me I can't pray?"

Other factors that impact teacher effectiveness are the quality of the school itself, the nature of the community that the school serves, the nature and degree of parental involvement, and the financial resources available to the school. Thus effective teaching is determined by a constellation of factors, the most important single factor being the teacher himself or herself. These other factors, however, significantly impact the overall effectiveness of the classroom teacher.

Another major criticism of teachers is that they work a shorter workday and work year than other professionals. There is some truth to this, but not as much as appears at first blush. Many teachers spend a good deal of time out of school preparing lessons, grading papers, and contacting parents. These activities typically require an extra hour or two a day, bringing the teacher workday into line with the norm in the general workforce. In addition, a fair percentage of teachers work with students for several hours after school supervising and coaching athletic teams or sponsoring other extracurricular events.

When done correctly, teaching is a physically and emotionally draining occupation. At an absolute minimum, the teacher is responsible for twenty-five children for many hours each day. The physical and psychic energy required for this degree of interpersonal interactions is greater than that experienced by many professionals in their typical work setting.

Studies indicate that many workers across virtually all occupations spend a significant part of their workday on activities not relating to their work. This can range from cell phone calls to friends to shopping on eBay to discussing last night's football game at the water cooler. Teachers engage in such activities to a lesser degree than other knowledge workers, given that they typically work as the sole adult supervising and instructing students in a self-contained classroom. In the chapter on international comparisons, chapter 18, we see that the workday of an American teacher is generally longer and more intense than in other developed countries.

The quality of the teaching force is also affected by larger societal factors. In previous generations, teaching was one of the few professions generally available to women. Over the past forty years, women have had many more career opportunities than previously and therefore many of the women who would have been excellent teachers in the past now pursue other careers.

In the late 1960s the proportion of men in the teaching profession rose as young men sought deferments from military service during the Vietnam War. Absent the draft, there has been a decline in young men seeking teaching careers in recent decades. The pool of potentially excellent teachers is smaller today for both men and women than was true forty years ago.

The supply problem is further exacerbated by the fact that the number of public school teachers has increased from about 2.1 million to more than 3 million over these four decades. This significant increase primarily reflects the increasing demand for special education teachers, reading specialists, and teacher coaches and mentors. There has also been a trend toward smaller class sizes, reflecting a student population that is increasingly diverse and requires more individual attention. Thus administrators must dip further into the pool of potential teachers to simply staff the schools, much less recruit an effective teacher for every classroom.

The problem of recruiting competent teachers is, of course, most daunting in the very underperforming schools most in need of excellent teachers. In many of our most challenging schools it is impossible to find teachers who are academically prepared and certified in the subject areas that they are asked to teach. Teacher turnover is another problem that is particularly acute in our underperforming schools.

On a national basis, close to 50 percent of new teachers leave their schools within five years. More than half leave the profession entirely, while the remaining teachers leave to work in other schools or districts. The general direction of this flow of younger teachers is from poorer school districts to more affluent school districts.

Thus, in addition to the challenges endemic to schools in lower socio-economic areas, the problems are exacerbated by high teacher turnover in schools already handicapped by many teachers that are not academically prepared to teach their assigned subjects.

Why is it that teaching, which too many critics assume is an easy occupation, manages to lose almost one-half of its new recruits over a five-year period? The answers in most cases are poor working conditions, lack of job satisfaction, and inadequate administrative support and mentoring. This is particularly true for the many teachers who must practice their profession in the dysfunctional schools in our inner cities and rural pockets of poverty. As mentioned previously, some of these young teachers do not actually leave the profession. They tend instead to migrate to school districts with better working conditions and a student and parent population that is more supportive and appreciative of their efforts.

Low salaries are not the major reason for the difficulty in attracting and retaining good teachers. While basic compensation could certainly benefit from being somewhat higher, we should recognize that most teachers in the United States enjoy high-quality fringe benefits and pensions. Couple this with the very small chance of layoff and unemployment throughout a thirty-five-year career, and one could convincingly argue that, over a lifetime, teacher compensation is not as meager as it may first appear.

Another work comparing education in six first-world countries, including the United States, found that the working conditions of teachers in the United

States tend to be far inferior to that of teachers in most of the other countries studied—Canada, England, Denmark, Germany, and Japan. The actual time that our teachers spend in direct instruction, as well as time required for non-professional duties such as lunch duty and study hall coverage, far exceeds the norm elsewhere (McAdams, 1993, 237).

In secondary schools abroad, for example, students are left to themselves during lunch and other break times far more than in our country. The United States is far more litigious than other nations; thus our students need to be more closely supervised by teachers than is the norm elsewhere.

All things considered, to what extent is a lack of teacher quality responsible for the deficiencies in public education? A shortage of qualified teachers in our inner cities, as well as nationwide in subject areas such as science and math, does represent critical problems. For the great majority of teachers nationwide, however, a lack of competence does not rise to the level of a serious problem.

While it is true that many elementary teachers lack an acceptable under-standing of the fundamental principles of science and math, these concepts can be taught effectively through rigorous staff development programs. Most elementary teachers in America can be taught these basic concepts at a level that can be transmitted effectively to elementary school students.

The most serious problems of teacher quality exist in our dysfunctional schools in our major cities. It is impossible in many cases to secure teach-ers who are minimally certified, much less qualified. Many teachers in these schools do have the qualifications and the desire to be effective teachers. Unfortunately, too many of them have simply been worn down over the years by the sometimes deplorable conditions under which they are expected to teach.

The major disincentives to teaching effectiveness in such schools are needy students, disengaged parents, an unsupportive school administration, deterio-rating physical facilities, and a lack of basic student discipline or even basic safety for students and teachers. An *Education Week* article in the June 16, 2010, issue, for example, reported that in Philadelphia 70 percent of violent students who committed felony assaults on teachers went unpunished (Stoll-steimer, 2010). All of these factors undermine a good learning environment. Such poor working conditions breed the militant unionism that, while provid-ing minimal protection to teachers, undermines the collegial working envi-ronment that would be conducive to a well-organized and functioning school.

In such situations a militant union is a symptom of deeper difficulties and is not itself the major problem. Chapter 4, "The Impact of Teachers Unions," addresses the role that teachers unions play in the effectiveness of America's public schools. This discussion demonstrates that, while unions are definitely not an advantage, they actually have a rather minor impact on the overall effectiveness of public schools in the United States.

In summary, the American teaching corps is doing good work under conditions that are often adverse. Although many consider teaching to be a relatively easy job, we have a chronic shortage of teachers in many geographic areas and in several subject areas. There are fairly simple solutions to these challenges, which are discussed in later chapters. We need to build on the foundation of the solid teaching corps that we already have.

2

Daily Life of a Teacher

$\mathbf{W}$alking in the shoes of another provides a quick education in life as it is lived by that person. In this chapter we explore teaching from the trenches. We see that the daily experience of teaching, while often exhilarating, can also be draining both physically and emotionally. The high attrition rate for young teachers becomes more readily understandable. A look at the work life of teachers in other countries provides further context for considering the daily life of a teacher in America.

The conventional wisdom about the teacher work year and workday is a distortion of reality. For example, consider the canard that teachers have a three-month vacation as compared with three weeks for the average worker. The typical teacher works about 190 days per year. Legal holidays and summer vacation are not counted as part of the work year.

The average American worker has about three weeks of vacation plus perhaps ten holidays. There are potentially 260 workdays in a year. Subtract fifteen for vacation time and ten for paid holidays and we see that the typical worker is on the job about 235 days per year. Thus teachers work about forty-five days, or nine weeks, less than the typical American worker. This is a substantial difference in favor of teachers, but not the thirteen weeks implied by the three-month vacation of popular lore.

At any given time about 20 percent of the teacher workforce attends evening or summer classes requiring substantial additional work effort. Teachers do not get paid directly for this investment of time and energy, but instead receive raises of perhaps $1,500 for every fifteen graduate credits that they earn. Thus a typical teacher must attend summer school for three years to get a rather modest salary increase of $1,000–$2,000. This increase does become part of base salary, so that over a long period the salary differential can be significant.

The typical teacher workday is about seven and one-half hours, including a thirty-minute lunch break. The teacher usually has about forty-five minutes per day of what is known as "planning time." This time is available for planning lessons; constructing and grading tests and student papers; preparing materials for class use; and meeting with colleagues, supervisors, or parents as required.

The rest of the day is spent working with and supervising groups of students. Simply supervising groups of twenty-five students at a time is a sufficient task in itself before considering the additional obligation to direct student energies in an academically productive fashion. Most teachers spend an additional one to two hours per day beyond the official workday in lesson planning and other school-related work.

Admittedly, some teachers devote little time to outside-of-school instructional planning. Some of these teachers adopt a minimalist attitude toward their work characteristic of less conscientious workers in all occupations. Others have taught the same material for many years and do not find it necessary to spend as much time in lesson preparation as previously. Perhaps 20 percent of teachers fall into this category.

However, there are teachers who typically spend considerable extra time each day perfecting their understanding of their material and working to develop more creative and effective ways to present the lesson. Probably about 20 percent of teachers fall into this category. The remaining 60 percent of teachers work the thirty-five- to forty-five-hour workweek common to workers in the general society.

A significant number of secondary school teachers also supervise extracurricular or cocurricular activities that require a few hours of time and effort after the regular student day. These activities include tasks as varied as being a football coach to serving as the faculty advisor to the school newspaper. Teachers typically receive supplemental contracts for such services. Such compensation often totals from $1,000–$3,000. On an hourly basis the extra compensation is typically in the $10–$15 range.

Speaking in terms of hours worked per day, week, or year only partially captures the nature of a teacher's work life. One interesting data point is that almost 50 percent of teachers leave the profession within five years. A partial explanation of this phenomenon is the modest salaries that teachers receive, especially early in their career. If they remain in the profession for fifteen or twenty years, their salary becomes more competitive with other professions. Fringe benefits, pension provisions, and job security begin to look much more attractive to teachers as they approach age forty, one reason that few teachers leave after reaching midcareer.

Most teachers exiting the profession, however, do so for reasons that are not monetary. One salient fact is that our society holds teachers in relatively low regard. This status deficit plays a significant role in the lack of job satisfaction felt by many teachers. Being well thought of by one's family and friends is a major factor in achieving the reasonable level of self-regard that we all seek.

Our opinion leaders often give lip service to the importance of teachers and the effect that individual teachers have had on their own lives. The general society, however, never translates this supposed high esteem into concrete steps to improve the financial status or working conditions of teachers. There are few upper- and middle-class parents who would encourage their children to pursue a teaching career. A large proportion of new teachers are first-generation college graduates who are mainly drawn from the lower middle class.

A column posted in *The Week* online on August 13, 2009, illustrates the reasons why young teachers leave the profession:

> I quit. After four years of teaching at a public charter school in Washington, D.C., I'm walking away from my students and my profession. Armed with high ideals and an Ivy League education, I became a teacher because I loved the idea of making a difference in young lives in urban school districts. Teaching was sometimes "exhilarating," but my best efforts to engage students from troubled families often failed.
>
> It was painful trying to reach students such as Shauna, a 10th grader who could barely read and had resolved that the best way to deal with me was to curse me out under her breath. But though I tell people that I'm burned out, my reason for leaving goes beyond simple frustration. I'm tired of giving my all for a profession that is widely viewed as "second-rate," fit only for people who lack the drive and intelligence to make it in business, medicine, or law.
>
> People like me are constantly asked, why teach? It's nice, "but it's not a real job." Largely because of that attitude, half of all new teachers quit within five years. Now I know why. (Fine, 2009)

The young woman quoted here is not truly representative of the average teacher. She is a graduate of an elite university, and she and her university peers may not identify with many of the helping professions, not just teachers. Furthermore, as a young Ivy League graduate, she undoubtedly has other opportunities more advantageous both in terms of salary and lifestyle than does the typical teacher. Many teachers are as frustrated as she is but don't have the opportunity to change careers. They may have limited financial resources, large student loans, or a family to support.

When such teachers find themselves in a dysfunctional school, their frustration can lead to a crippling level of cynicism and disillusionment. These teachers who literally feel trapped in their lives as teachers are the individuals who become cynical and withdrawn as they reach midcareer. Of course, many midcareer people in all occupations feel disengaged from their work. In many occupations, such lack of enthusiasm does not detract greatly from job performance. Effectively teaching young people, however, requires teachers who remain energetic and engaged throughout their career.

Forty or more years ago a teacher didn't need to endure a sixteen-year-old smart aleck cursing at her under her breath on a regular basis. The child would be sent to the principal, would receive a detention if not a suspension, and would be removed from the class if the student refused to behave in a civil manner. Having to repeatedly submit to the kind of disrespect described by Ms. Fine undermines the self-respect of the teacher.

While public school teaching may not be the most difficult job in the world, it is more challenging than most other occupations. Let's look at a typical day for both a high school teacher and an elementary school teacher. Most high schools start the school day comparatively early in the morning, about 7:30 a.m. This is partially because a few hours need to be available at the end of the school day for athletic and cocurricular activities, as well as to enable students to pursue part-time jobs.

The day typically begins with a twenty-minute homeroom period where attendance is taken, announcements are made, and routine administrative tasks are performed. The teachers and students then begin a seven- or eight-period marathon with class periods of forty to forty-five minutes, bracketed by three- to four-minute breaks to move from class to class. Teachers and students also have a thirty-minute lunch period. The unlucky ones may have lunch as early as 10:30 a.m. or as late as 1:00 p.m.

The typical high school teacher delivers instruction for five, or perhaps six, of these class periods. Teaching assignments involve two or three different lesson preparations delivered to students across two or more grade levels. Many of the classes are ability-grouped, meaning that the conscientious teacher must tailor the instruction to each class in terms of academic ability as well as subject and grade level. In situations where ability grouping is not used, the teacher has fewer formal preparations, but must make accommodations in each class for the various ability and interest levels of her students.

The teacher is allotted about forty-five minutes during the workday to prepare these varied lessons; prepare materials for class; and meet with parents, students, and supervisors as required. It should be apparent that for a teacher to do justice to his or her responsibilities requires additional time each day beyond the seven-and-one-half-hour official workday. Teachers who do not put in the extra time, and there are too many of them, cannot provide the excellent instructional product that we all seek.

The miracle is that so many teachers do make extraordinary efforts, without recognition or recompense, to make the attempt to be excellent teachers. These teachers are true heroes in our society. These are the same teachers who maintain their enthusiasm and love of students throughout their teaching career. There are many more such teachers than we have a right to expect.

Elementary school teachers have a similar seven-and-one-half-hour official workday. These teachers are with their students from roughly 8:15 a.m. until 3:45 p.m., except for a forty-five-minute planning period and a thirty-minute lunch period. The academic content for the subjects taught in elementary school is obviously not difficult. Nonetheless, these teachers must prepare five or six separate lessons each day. The challenge is to present often-complex information to young children in an intellectually compelling manner.

Also, at least for math and language arts, the elementary teacher must prepare several versions of the math and language arts lesson for the different levels of ability in her class. She or he typically has class sizes of about twenty-five. Interestingly, teachers of the more academically motivated students in wealthier school districts have smaller classes of perhaps twenty, while their colleagues in the schools of our inner cities often have thirty or more students per class.

Elementary teachers, particularly in the lower grades, must review a large number of student practice sheets in math and reading on a daily basis. In the upper elementary grades teachers also have science and social studies projects to evaluate. These tasks are in addition to regular tests that need to be graded.

Most elementary teachers work one to three hours in the evening or late afternoon to complete these out-of-class obligations. Teachers also interact far more frequently with the parents of their young children than do their secondary school counterparts. These parental contacts have increased geometrically with the advent of e-mail. Secondary teachers probably spend similar amounts of time on parent contacts, given that they teach between 125 and 150 students each day as compared with the twenty-five students in an elementary school class.

In recent decades, the pressures on teachers have increased in two major respects. Children have become less docile than in previous generations, while parents have become more insistent that their children be treated with the highest degree of understanding and sensitivity. The days are long gone when parents would routinely tell their students that the teacher is always right. Meanwhile, school district administrators, state officials, and the media have become more insistent that all students perform at a higher level. These sometimes contradictory expectations place more pressures on teachers than was the case in previous decades.

The ever-increasing insistence on higher achievement levels for students makes it necessary for teachers to be more demanding, while parents often assert counterpressures on teachers. Parents often complain that their students are given too much homework or that there is too much performance pressure placed on their children. It also seems likely that the present-day parent, often heading a single-parent household, simply has less time and energy to help a student with schoolwork than back in the days when two parents, including a stay-at-home mom, was the norm.

There is a common assumption that if teachers simply try harder, student achievement will increase dramatically. The brief review of the frenetic pace of the typical teacher's workday demonstrates that teachers barely have enough time to adequately prepare for their classes. There is little time to reflect on the effectiveness of one's teaching, to interact with other teachers to try to improve instructional strategies, or even to analyze why students are not performing better. Nor is there time to analyze why achievement improves when it does improve.

Teachers in Japan have an activity known as "polishing the stone." This means that Japanese teachers collaborate with one another to improve instruction, conduct sample classes that are reviewed by colleagues, and evaluate the success of the strategies that they are using. The book *Lessons from Abroad* (McAdams, 1993) compared the work life of teachers in six industrialized countries. American teachers typically spend from twenty-two to twenty-seven hours per week in direct student instructional contact time, with additional time spent on supervisory duties such as cafeteria duty or study hall monitor.

This compares with fifteen to twenty hours per week of student instructional time with no supervisory duties in countries such as Japan, Denmark, and Germany. This is a very significant difference totaling two hundred to three hundred hours over the course of a school year. Japanese teachers spend much of this extra time "polishing the stone" in an effort to improve instruction. Teachers in Canada and England have instructional teaching loads similar to those in the United States.

Another finding from *Lessons from Abroad* is that American teachers are far more likely than their counterparts in the other countries to hold part-time jobs during the school year. Such jobs often divert teachers from investing available time and energy to improving their teaching performance. Teachers generally hold part-time jobs in the first half of their careers, when their salaries are still relatively low and they are struggling financially to form households and raise children. The debt burden from college loans is also a factor for American teachers. Many other countries subsidize a far larger proportion of college costs than is the norm in the United States.

To bring student contact hours in the United States down to the level of Japan, Denmark, and Germany would require an increase in the teacher cadre of about 20 percent. This option is cost-prohibitive in an environment where school costs are already high by historical standards. Chapter 16, "School Finance," provides explanations for this relatively high cost of education in the United States that have little to do with the core teaching and learning process.

Another possible strategy to create more teacher planning time is to increase average class sizes by five students, from about twenty-five to thirty. This would only be practical if we were to return to a more docile student body and fewer demands from parents for individualizing and customizing instruction. Our modern cultural expectations for parenting and schooling would need to change, an unlikely scenario. If this second option were politically possible, it could be achieved at relatively little additional cost.

This chapter has demonstrated that American teachers lead a frenetic work life with little time available to prepare their lessons at an optimal level. Working conditions in many schools are inferior to those enjoyed by other professional-level workers. Some teachers succumb to these circumstances by either leaving the profession or by morphing into mediocre performers as they approach midcareer and beyond.

Thankfully, most teachers internalize the satisfaction that they obtain from working successfully with students and helping them achieve the skills and values that will form decent and productive adults. These teachers overcome the barriers to providing a solid educational experience to students and represent the abiding strength of American public schools. In chapter 19, "Final Exam," we explore possible strategies for improving the daily work experiences of our teachers.

3

Demographic Changes and Student Achievement

In gauging the effectiveness of public schools, we must first consider the context of demographic factors influencing our public school students and their teachers. We explore the changing demographics of public school students over the decades. We also compare student achievement data over the decades in the United States as well as comparative achievement data on an international basis. Throughout this chapter, numbers are rounded for ease of discussion and understanding. Base years vary in different data comparisons depending upon the source of the data.

The first item to explore is the number of students attending school in 1969 compared with 2008. In 1969 there were 45.6 million public school children and 5.5 million private and parochial school students. Thus approximately 89 percent of students attended public schools while 11 percent attended private or parochial schools. In 2008 approximately 49.8 million children attended public school while 6.1 million attended private and parochial schools. These 2008 data indicate that 89 percent of students attended public schools while 11 percent attended private and parochial schools (Snyder, Dillow, and Hoffman, 2009, 16).

The percentages have remained quite stable over this forty-year period despite frequent assertions by opinion leaders that people are losing faith in their public schools. Of the number of public school students reported in 2008, about 1.4 million (3 percent) of students attended charter schools. Although they operate independently of public schools, charter schools are considered part of the public school system because they receive public funds.

At least three factors can account for the surprisingly stable percentage of students attending public schools throughout this forty-year period. This is somewhat counterintuitive since over this time period the public schools have been consistently described as "mediocre" or worse. Countless books and reports have highlighted the deficiencies of the public schools, the alleged doleful effects of teachers unions, and the lack of proper financing and accountability.

Each year the Gallup organization conducts a poll of public attitudes toward public schools. Public approval of the schools has generally declined over the past thirty years. By 2008 parents assigned a grade of midway between a B and a C to the public schools attended by their own students. Adults without children in the schools rated their community schools a bit lower. When asked to grade schools on a national basis, the grades assigned were lower still (Snyder et al., 2009, 42).

The first factor accounting for the stability in the proportion of students attending public schools is that although inner-city Catholic schools have closed by the hundreds in recent decades, affecting hundreds of thousands of students, today a similar number of students are either homeschooled or attend charter schools. There is some evidence that in many urban areas both Catholic and non-Catholic parents, who in prior decades would have sent their children to Catholic schools, now send them to charter schools (Ravitz, 2010, 128).

A second factor is that today a smaller percentage of parents of public school children can afford to send their children to private schools than in previous decades. As we will see, a large proportion of public school children come from poverty-level homes—families that would find it difficult, if not impossible, to afford private or parochial school tuition.

In 1959 more than seventeen million children lived below the poverty line. By 2007 the overall number of children below the poverty line had fallen to just under thirteen million. While the number of white children living below the poverty line declined from 11.2 million to just under 4 million, the number of black and Hispanic students below the poverty line rose from 6.6 million to about 8.2 million. Today approximately 18 percent of children under eighteen live in families below the poverty line.

The breakdown of children in poverty by race indicates that 10 percent of white children, 34 percent of black children, and 28 percent of Hispanic children live below the poverty level (Snyder et al., 2009, 39–41).

While the proportion of black and Hispanic students living in poverty is much higher than that of white students, the absolute numbers of such students in each ethnic group paints a different picture. In 2007 the numbers of students living in poverty by race was as follows: 4 million white children, 3.8 million black children, and 4.3 million Hispanic children. Thus, in terms of the number of students negatively affected by poverty, each of the three major ethnic groups is similarly afflicted. We can assume that these numbers have risen significantly during the recent economic downturn.

The third factor is that private and charter schools are simply not an option for the thousands of school districts nationwide where students are more geographically dispersed than in our major cities or inner-ring suburbs. Arriving at a critical mass of students within a reasonable busing distance of a charter or private school is simply not feasible for perhaps 50 percent of our public school population nationally.

Another major demographic shift over the past decades is in the significantly greater number of students who live in single-parent homes. In 1970 approximately 25.5 million families with children under eighteen were composed of married-couple homes. At that time an additional 3.2 million families lived in single-parent households.

In 2007 there were twenty-six million married-couple families with children under eighteen. There were, however, 10.6 million single-parent families. This represents more than a threefold increase in single-parent households over the decades. Digging deeper into the data reveals that approximately seventeen million children under age eighteen currently live in single-parent households (Snyder et al., 2009, 35).

Today, about one-fourth of children under age eighteen live in single-parent households. A recent report indicated that in 2008, 40 percent of babies were born into a one-parent household, foreshadowing a substantially larger proportion of children of single parents attending public schools in the near future. Although many single parents do an excellent job raising their children, there is no question that raising and educating a child successfully is generally more difficult in a single-parent household. All of the challenges associated with rearing children fall to one adult who is often more constrained in both time and economic resources than the typical two-parent family.

Another dramatic change in the student population over the last forty years concerns the number of students who speak English as a second language (ESL). These ESL students vary in their English proficiency from those who speak and read the language fluently to many who speak little or no English. Of the eleven million students who speak another language, almost three million have difficulty speaking English with fluency (Planty et al., 2009, 18–19).

Even those who speak English very well are nonetheless somewhat challenged given that English is not their native tongue. These eleven million students represent approximately 20 percent of the public school population. As recently as 1980 there were fewer than four million students who spoke a language other than English at home.

A final major change in the demographic of public school students involves the growing number of students identified as needing special education services. There is no doubt that prior to the passage of the Individuals with Disabilities Education Act in 1975, students with special needs were being underserved by our schools. There also is some evidence that the number of students with special needs has increased partially due to environmental, social, or medical factors affecting the student population.

For a variety of reasons, the number of students receiving special educational services has increased from 3.7 million in 1976 to 6.7 million in 2007 (Planty et al., 2009, 20). Providing these special services to 13 percent of public school students has complicated the educational mission of the schools and has significantly increased the cost of schooling, as we shall see in chapter 15, "Special Education and Other Special Services."

Considering these demographic factors, we find that substantial minorities of public school students arrive at the schoolhouse door with a variety of challenges and handicaps to learning. These data indicate that approximately 18 percent of public school students live below the poverty line, more than 25 percent of public school students reside in single-parent households, 20 percent of students live in homes where English is not the native language, and about 13 percent of students require special education services.

Experiencing three or four of these factors represents a combination of circumstances that dramatically increases the probability that these students will perform poorly in school. Having large numbers of such students in the same school greatly magnifies the challenges facing teachers and administrators—no matter how competent and dedicated.

It is safe to say that nationally at least one-fourth of our public school students present the schools with significant educational challenges. The situation is exacerbated by the fact that students saddled with multiple educational and social disadvantages tend to be concentrated in our major cities and in poor, rural areas such as Appalachia.

Many people mistakenly believe that education is something that educators can simply inject into the student. More than in other professional interactions, the teacher requires the cooperation and active participation of the student for learning to occur. A doctor can treat a patient successfully if the patient simply submits to the treatment. A lawyer can successfully prosecute a legal case with a minimum of direct input from the client. Teaching success, however, is heavily dependent on the quality of the interactions between a competent teacher and a capable and cooperative learner.

When one-fourth of the student body arrives at school ill-equipped to participate actively in the learning process, the task of the teacher becomes infinitely more difficult. Inadequate training to assist teachers in their work with these special populations further complicates the teacher's task.

Conventional wisdom about American schools is that they are performing poorly and are probably becoming worse over time. Both of these assumptions are false. This is not to say that the level of student performance is satisfactory or could not be improved. The following data indicate that student performance has actually improved somewhat over the past forty years and that although our performance on international achievement tests is usually reported in a bad light, the performance of our students is actually quite respectable.

A few caveats before delving into standardized testing data and its inter-pretation. We will assume for the sake of discussion that these data are valid in the sense that they accurately portray student achievement on material that is actually taught in our schools—this may not be a totally valid assumption.

We also don't want to assume that concerning ourselves with mainly math and reading skills offers a comprehensive view of educational achievement. Education is and should be concerned with many topics and subjects in addition to basic skills. In reality, basic skills achievement is important because it makes possible the acquisition of knowledge and skills in other areas of the curriculum.

The National Assessment of Educational Progress (NAEP) is a national as-sessment test administered to a sample of U.S. students every few years. The first testing was done in 1971 and the most recent available testing results are from 2008. The tests are given to American students at ages nine, thirteen, and seventeen. So-called scaled scores are reported because they are the most accurate statistically in comparing scores among students across time.

The average scaled scores for students in mathematics at each testing across this thirty-five-year period are shown in table 3.1.

Table 3.1. National Trends in Mathematics by Average Scale Score

	1973	1978	1982	1986	1990	1994	1999	2004	2008
Age 9	219	219	219	222	230	231	232	241	243
Age 13	266	264	269	269	270	274	276	281	281
Age 17	304	300	298	302	305	306	308	307	306

Source: Rampey, B. D., Dion, G. S., and Donahue, P. L. (2009). *NAEP 2008 Trends in Academic Progress in Reading and Mathematics* (NCES 2009-479). National Center for Education Statistics, Institute of Educa-tion Sciences, U.S. Department of Education, Washington, DC.

While we do not see dramatic changes in these math scores over the years, there is a slight drift upward, most pronounced with nine-year-old students and least pronounced with seventeen-year-old students.

Similar data for students in reading over a thirty-three-year period are shown in table 3.2.

Table 3.2. National Trends in Reading by Average Scale Score

	1975	1980	1984	1988	1992	1996	1999	2004	2008
Age 9	210	215	211	212	211	212	212	219	220
Age 13	256	258	257	257	260	258	259	259	260
Age 17	286	285	289	290	290	288	288	283	286

Source: Rampey, B. D., Dion, G. S., and Donahue, P. L. (2009). *NAEP 2008 Trends in Academic Progress in Reading and Mathematics* (NCES 2009-479). National Center for Education Statistics, Institute of Educa-tion Sciences, U.S. Department of Education, Washington, DC.

Once again we see a very gentle upward slope over time, although less pronounced than the gains with math scores. Since reading scores are thought to be more affected by the home environment than math scores, researchers believe that math scores are a better measure of pure school effects. Also, one theory holds that performance changes tend to be greater at younger ages because younger students are less susceptible to negative external environmental factors than are their older brothers and sisters.

Another caveat is that the test data for seventeen-year-old students obviously reflects only those students who still attend school. In many of our inner cities, a large number of students have dropped out of school, and their scores, which one can assume would be weak, are not reflected in the data.

The unbelievably high absentee rate among students in some of our disadvantaged communities provides a truly sobering statistic. It is axiomatic that students can't learn if they are not physically present in school. In many schools in these communities, as many as 20 percent of students are absent on any given day. This means that the average student in these schools is absent almost 40 out of 180 school days each year.

This is the average! Some students are absent sixty, eighty, or more than one hundred days each year. Student absences of this magnitude are not usually a matter of simple indifference. Students in these communities sometimes lack a primary caregiver, are affected by drug or alcohol abuse, or cannot face more failure at school.

An additional factor depressing student performance in many inner-city schools is the high turnover in the student population. In most rural and suburban school districts there might be a 10 percent turnover of the student body in a given year. In many urban school districts the student turnover rate is 30 percent or more. There are some inner-city schools where student turnover is 100 percent or more in a school year. This turnover rate matters because students moving from one school to another need to adjust to a new environment, new teachers, new friends, and somewhat different instructional strategies if not new curricula. All of these factors serve as an impediment to good student performance.

A superintendent in a school district with a high percentage of disadvantaged students asked a fifth-grade class how many of them had attended this school since first grade. Only two students out of the twenty-five in class that day answered in the affirmative. A depressingly high number of students in such communities change schools several times within a single school year. This constant turnover among students is a major problem for the teachers as well as the students.

It is impossible to argue from these data that educational achievement in the United States has been declining over the past several decades. Instead, there has been modest progress. This progress is in spite of the data on student demographics that indicate a much higher proportion of at-risk students in the public school population than in the past. The dramatic increase in non-English speakers in the school population has certainly negatively impacted student performance.

Also note that a high proportion of today's public school students come from single-parent households—a generally negative influence on student performance. The data demonstrate that there has been some improvement in student achievement in the face of an increasingly challenging student population.

In chapter 16, "School Finance," we will see that per-pupil expenditures over the past decades have more than doubled in constant dollars. Thus public school critics sometimes argue that we have paid a very high price for the slight improvements that we have experienced. Once we dig into the financial details, however, we will see why such additional investments have led to comparatively low educational payoffs.

INTERNATIONAL COMPARISONS OF STUDENT ACHIEVEMENT

In spite of the increasing challenges facing our students, the overall performance of our public schools is marginally better than it was a generation or two ago. The following section summarizes performance data from international comparisons of education.

By looking at longitudinal data from NAEP, we have been able to track student achievement in the United States over more than a thirty-year period. This gives us a now-versus-then comparison where we have seen small but positive improvements in student achievement. To make here-versus-there comparisons, we turn to data from the Trends in International Math and Science Study (TIMSS) from 2007.

The comparison of fourth- and eighth-grade student performance in science is conducted every four years. The 2007 study included thirty-six countries at the fourth-grade level and forty-eight countries at the eighth-grade level. Scaled scores were used (TIMSS average = 500) to compare student performance in countries throughout the world.

Countries volunteer to participate in the study and typically do so when they believe that the curriculum in their country corresponds closely to that tested by the TIMSS instrument. Some countries that do participate are later disqualified from the study if the TIMSS officials believe that the sampling procedures used in a given country were not valid. These factors introduce some reliability and validity concerns into international testing instruments such as TIMSS.

In fourth-grade science in 2007 students in four countries performed significantly better than U.S. students (Singapore, Chinese Taipei, Hong Kong–Special Administrative Region of China [SAR], and Japan). Six countries had scores similar to scores of U.S. students (Russian Federation, Latvia, England, Hungary, Italy, and Kazakhstan). Twenty-five countries had scores that were significantly lower than those of U.S. students. Some of the more highly developed of these countries with lower scores include Germany, Australia, Sweden, Netherlands, Denmark, Czech Republic, Scotland, and Norway.

At the eighth-grade level in science, students in eight countries performed significantly better than U.S. students (Singapore, Chinese Taipei, Japan, Republic of Korea, England, Hungary, Czech Republic, and Slovenia). Four countries achieved average scores similar to those of U.S. students (Hong Kong–SAR, Lithuania, Russian Federation, and Australia). Students in thirty-five countries achieved scores that were significantly lower than the scores of U.S. students. Some of the more highly developed countries among the thirty-five countries with lower scores than American students include Sweden, Scotland, Italy, Norway, and Israel (Martin et al., 2008, 34–35).

Similar results occurred at the fourth- and eighth-grade levels in the TIMSS 2007 mathematics scores. American fourth graders scored eleventh of thirty-six countries in the study. American eighth grade students scored ninth of forty-eight countries (Mullis et al., 2008, 34–35). Interesting data from the TIMSS 2007 Mathematics study indicates that students in Massachusetts ranked fourth of thirty-six countries at the fourth-grade level and students in Minnesota rankled fifth of thirty-six countries on this test (Mullis et al., 2008, 34). In fact, Massachusetts fourth graders ranked second worldwide in science and first worldwide in science at the eighth-grade level.

American students generally perform poorly on the Program for International Student Assessment (PISA) tests administered to a sample of fifteen-year-old students from twenty-nine Organization for Economic Cooperation and Development (OECD) countries. On the whole, these twenty-nine countries are among the most economically developed in the world. In mathematics literacy American fifteen-year-old students ranked twenty-fifth of twenty-nine countries.

American students ranked seventeenth of twenty-nine countries in science literacy. Twenty-seven additional countries participated in these tests. American student performance compared with these twenty-seven countries tended to be better than the comparisons among the twenty-nine OECD countries (Snyder et al., 2009, 578).

A more positive international comparison can be found in the results of the 2006 Progress in International Reading Literacy Study (PIRLS) administered to fourth-grade students in forty-one countries. At a scaled score of 540, the American students scored well above the international average score of 500. American students earned scores that ranked them fifteenth of the forty-one countries in the study (Mullis et al., 2007, 37).

Of the fourteen countries with higher average scores than the United States, only eight had scores that were significantly higher. By racial and ethnic background, the average scores for American students were as follows: Asian (567), white (560), Hispanic (518), black (503), and American Indian/Alaska Native (468).

We can speculate about the reasons for the generally poorer performance of our high school students on international tests compared with the generally better performance of our students at the fourth- and eighth-grade levels. Perhaps our high school students realize that mediocre academic performance will not be a bar to attending college. Many other countries have more restrictive access to higher education at least partially influenced by student performance on externally developed exit exams.

Perhaps our students are distracted by the American culture and teenage lifestyle to a greater degree than foreign students in their own cultures. Perhaps our desire to have all students succeed leads to less of an academic press in schools serving our less academically oriented students.

Taking this point from the abstract to the particular, let us consider two eleventh-grade math teachers in two very different high schools. The first school has moderately rigorous academic standards. Parents see that their children attend school regularly, do their homework, and participate in class. In this situation perhaps a few students will not actively engage in classroom activities. When these students do poorly, compared with the majority of more motivated students, the onus for failure is on these few students rather than on the teacher. The teacher can rightly point out that her instruction is effective with the great majority of her students.

Our second teacher labors in a school with a high level of student absenteeism, little parental support, and a majority of students who are both disengaged and lacking the necessary math background to succeed in her class. Most of her students fail their tests, do not complete assignments, and constantly ask that the teacher review material that students miss due to absenteeism.

In an environment where pressure is put on the teachers to move students toward graduation, the onus for failure is on the teacher. After all, she must be ineffective if large numbers of her students are failing the course. Students from such schools naturally perform poorly on standardized tests and compare poorly with their peers across the country and around the world.

An underlying assumption in analyzing international test results is that the curriculum in the country being measured corresponds closely to the material tested on the international instruments. To the extent that the curriculum in a given country varies from the material tested, students in these countries will earn lower scores than if the curriculum tested corresponded closely to the taught curriculum. We see in chapter 11, "The Limits of Local Control," that curriculum decisions in the United States are made at the state and local levels, providing opportunity for greater variation in the taught curriculum in the United States than in countries with stronger national control over curriculum.

There is a growing movement in the United States for either national academic standards or more closely aligned standards from state to state. Presumably academic standards that are more uniform nationally will also be better aligned to the material tested on international comparison instruments. Better performance by American students would follow naturally if such national standards were better aligned with international testing instruments.

At both the fourth- and eighth-grade levels, on average across countries, higher mathematics achievement was associated with the following factors:

- Students speaking the language of the test at home
- Parental education levels
- Students attending schools with fewer students from economically disadvantaged homes
- Students attending schools with few attendance problems
- Positive teacher reports on the adequacy of teacher working conditions
- Student perception of being safe at school
- Principals and teachers reporting a positive view of school climate (Mullis et al., 2008, 7–8)

Americans like to think of themselves as "number one." In the case of international educational achievements, we clearly are not number one. On the major benchmarks for international comparisons (TIMSS, PIRLS, and PISA), we typically achieve a middling ranking. We also experience outlier results much lower than the average score in some studies (PISA fifteen-year-old math results) and much better than average on other measures (TIMSS fourth-grade science).

A thorough review of international test results from the 1990s demonstrates that American students performed rather well compared with their international peers. This study compared student performance on six international tests involving four subject areas (reading, mathematics, science, and civics) across four different grade levels. The study reported that "overall, U.S. students score somewhat higher than their peers in other industrialized nations, with only 19 percent of other nations scoring significantly higher and 38 percent significantly lower" (Boe and Shin, 2005, 688–695).

On balance, American student performance is respectable considering the large and growing proportion of at-risk students included in the American student population. While every country has a certain percentage of disadvantaged students, the social safety net in most other nations is more comprehensive than that in the United States.

We saw earlier in this chapter that at least one-fourth of American public school students are disadvantaged in one or more areas such as limited English speaking, learning disabilities, poverty level, and living in single-parent households. These students are concentrated in urban and rural areas where the public schools are underfunded and critically deficient in multiple respects.

The eighth-grade NAEP mathematics assessment from 2007 disaggregates student scores by major ethnic groups. On this test the average score was 297 for Asian and Pacific Islanders, 291 for white students, 265 for Hispanic students, 264 for American Indian/Alaska Native students, and 260 for black students (Grigg and Dion, 2007, 26).

Average scale scores in NAEP mathematics for fourth-grade students by eligibility for the National School Lunch Program and race or ethnicity in 2007 are shown in table 3.3.

Table 3.3.   NAEP 2007 Reading Scores by Eligibility for National School Lunch Program

Race or Ethnicity	Eligible	Not Eligible	No Eligibility Data
White	215	235	237
Black	198	216	214
Hispanic	199	217	219
Asian	217	239	238
American Indian/ Alaska Native	195	219	211

Source: U.S. Department of Education, Institute of Education Sciences, National Center for Education Statistics, National Assessment of Educational Progress (NAEP), 2007 Reading Assessment.

These results indicate clearly that, within racial groups, test performance is related to poverty levels. Further, on average, Asian students perform highest, followed by white students, who fare better than black and Hispanic students. Most educators believe that these disparities are largely a reflection of the socioeconomic milieu in which many minority students and at-risk white students find themselves. A combination of inferior schools and a poor safety net lead to significantly poorer performance among our most disadvantaged youth.

Reviewing the data from this chapter we can draw several conclusions:

- Student performance in America's public schools has actually improved somewhat over time.
- We do not have a systemic problem with America's public schools, but rather a critical problem with our schools located in areas of high poverty and concentrations of at-risk students.
- Our performance on international tests would improve if we address the problems in our poorest performing schools. There is no need to make large-scale changes in the majority of our one hundred thousand individual schools in the United States.
- The number of students poorly served by our schools has reached a critical mass of at least one-fourth of all American students. As a practical matter, leaving the moral imperative aside, our nation cannot prosper when one-fourth of our human capital is effectively sentenced to academic, economic, and social failure.
- The lack of a more uniform national curriculum puts American students at a disadvantage when compared to students in nations that have a common curriculum that is aligned with the international tests.

One further point about student performance should be addressed. During the past forty years, public school critics have repeatedly claimed that if the schools did not improve dramatically, our competitiveness with other nations would suffer. In spite of the perceived failings of our schools, the United States still leads the world in productivity, creativity, and innovation (International Comparison of Productivity, 2008, 1).

Our continued dominance in these areas is often attributed to "the American spirit" or to the "wonders of our capitalistic and entrepreneurial economy." This is no doubt true, but we can be sure that had our productivity fallen over the decades, the blame would have been placed squarely on the schools.

This brief overview of student performance in America's public schools allows for a cautiously optimistic outlook for the future. Although surely our schools can be much improved, generally speaking they have still served our society rather well over the past several decades.

In the following chapters we explore the major initiatives that have been both proposed and enacted to improve our schools and explain why each of them has had little or no success. There is no silver bullet that will quickly and inexpensively educate all of our children to the level that they deserve. There are, however, solutions to the challenges facing our nation's schools. Many of our schools can be improved with rather straightforward and inexpensive reforms.

These solutions include changes in the school calendar, curriculum alignment on a national basis, and exit exams for all students. More critically, there are solutions for the schools attended by our most disadvantaged students that could be implemented if we have the societal will to do so.

4

The Impact of Teachers Unions

The modern-day image of militant teachers unions can be traced to Albert Shanker's tenure as president of the New York City United Federation of Teachers. He led the New York City teachers on two illegal teacher strikes in 1967 and 1968, a step that shocked the nation at that time. Teachers unions in many districts and states over the next decade, particularly the industrial northeast, began to carry out illegal strikes or use their political influence to change state laws so as to permit teacher strikes.

By the early 1970s most states had passed laws allowing for teacher strikes under certain conditions. During the decade of the 1970s local school districts in the United States experienced several hundred teacher strikes each year. Powerful statewide unions developed in many states that were able to control legislation relating to teachers, and to bring the muscle of the state union power to bear on local negotiations in thousands of local school districts.

Many of the judgments in this chapter are based on direct knowledge of operations in seven school districts as well as interactions with colleagues in more than one hundred school districts over many years. Statements about the impact of teachers unions cannot be applied universally, but can be considered as representative of conditions in most areas.

Local school boards were no match for the state union representatives schooled in labor and negotiations tactics. Within a relatively few years, thousands of school districts found themselves with complex labor contracts that complicated, if not directly interfered with, the efficient operation of the schools. While some gains were made in basic teacher salaries, the major costs of the new labor contracts lay in the fringe benefits, staffing requirements, and class size limitations that found their way into negotiated agreements.

School boards, unfamiliar with negotiations and the daily operation of schools, made concessions at the bargaining table that complicated the management prerogatives of school administrators. Elaborate rules became enshrined in labor contracts, complicating procedures involving teacher assignments, curriculum development, teacher evaluations, and grievance procedures.

These requirements interfere with operating schools in the best interest of students and handcuff administrators in their efforts to provide quality instruction. The more elaborate the provisions in a given labor contract, the more pronounced is the negative effect on educational quality. Fortunately, the worst of such detrimental provisions exist in only a minority of districts nationwide.

At the state level, the powerful unions were able to secure passage of new laws that benefited teachers and often increased the burden of pensions on the general taxpayer. These advantages were often well hidden from the average voter and thus were favored by politicians who needed to court the unions but didn't wish to antagonize the taxpayer.

Unsustainable levels of public employee pension commitments, including those of teachers, are now a major cause of state budget problems during an economic downturn. In many states, the pension funds for teachers and other public employees are simply unsustainable in the long run. Some states with the greatest pension funding problems include California, New York, and New Jersey.

In time, the influence of teachers unions over grievance procedures, arbitration rulings, and state laws greatly enhanced the position of teachers vis-à-vis school administrators, school boards, parents, and the general public. This growing influence of teachers unions was most strongly felt in big cities that, as we have seen, were then and are now the site of our most challenging school performance problems. Thus the strong teachers unions in our large cities exacerbated and complicated the already herculean task of educating students in these schools.

In spite of the militancy noted previously, about one-third of states still do not require, but do permit, collective bargaining by teachers. There are also a handful of states where collective bargaining by teachers is specifically forbidden by statute. Even in states where powerful teachers unions successfully lobby the state legislature, there are many local school districts where the relationship between the state union and the local chapter is tenuous at best.

Taking the nation as a whole, probably about 25 percent of students attend school districts with very powerful teachers unions. Perhaps another 25 percent attend school districts with moderately influential teachers unions. The balance of America's students attends schools where the teachers union is but a minor influence on school operations and policies. In reality, the oft-cited criticism that teachers unions negatively affect school operations actually applies to a minority of our school districts.

The major criticism of teachers unions is that they protect incompetent teachers from being fired. An antiunion website features statistics that indicate that only a minute percentage of teachers get dismissed either as probationary teachers or as tenured teachers. In New Jersey only forty-seven tenured teachers were terminated over a ten-year period. The City of Los Angeles terminates an average of eleven teachers each year out of forty-three thousand tenured teachers. In Illinois, Chicago excluded, an average of two teachers out of ninety-five thousand tenured teachers are terminated each year (Center for Union Facts, 2010).

It is certainly true that in states with militant teachers unions it is nearly impossible to successfully fire a teacher. The cost and time required to dismiss a teacher are incredibly burdensome. The time and effort required of school administrators in such situations, not to mention the emotional strain, are such that only the most intrepid administrators will undertake the burden. The most affected, however, are the students who must submit to instruction by these teachers.

Another factor, however, sheds a different light on the problem of removing incompetent teachers. Almost one-half of all new teachers leave the profession within five years. The unstated assumption is that virtually all of these departures are of competent teachers who are leaving voluntarily. Behind-the-scenes encouragement from principals and colleagues, however, may be responsible for as many as one-third of these resignations.

A major source for these voluntary separations is the teacher himself or herself. If, for example, a teacher is unable to control a class, does not have the respect of his or her students, and receives constant complaints from parents and supervisors, wouldn't such a teacher be likely to voluntarily change professions? Perhaps as many as 25 percent of teachers who leave teaching voluntarily do so because they either cannot or will not perform satisfactorily. To maintain their own self-esteem, they will often tell themselves, families, and friends that they were not supported by their administrators or that they found the students to be undisciplined and the parents uncooperative.

This is certainly a common experience of new teachers in our most dysfunctional schools. It is very unrewarding and frustrating for teachers to spend every day in a situation where they are unsuccessful. This type of negative teaching experience is less common in well-functioning school districts where young teachers are better supported and more appreciated by parents and students.

Many teachers leaving the profession do not do so solely of their own volition. These are teachers who are ineffective but don't realize the extent of their shortcomings. In most such cases, their administrators will try to assist and coach the teacher. If remediation attempts are not successful, the administrator will try to counsel the teacher out of the profession.

Such counseling attempts are not the subject of grievance procedures or dismissal hearings, but nonetheless represent an effective means to separate unsuccessful teachers from the ranks. Some administrators are very adept at working with such teachers over the course of a year or so and ultimately bringing them to the point where they agree to resign voluntarily.

In many school districts there are even circumstances in which the teachers union itself tries to counsel unsatisfactory teachers out of the profession. While the union will defend the teacher in a formal sense, behind the scenes teacher colleagues and union officials will encourage the teacher to resign. Clearly, in some cases, this is to the advantage of both the union and the schools. Incompetent teachers hurt the reputation of teaching as a profession and make it more difficult for such teacher groups to maintain the support of the greater community—a valuable commodity during contract negotiations.

This collaborative dynamic is least likely to occur in dysfunctional school systems in many of our large cities and elsewhere. Teachers in such districts must deal with recalcitrant students, antagonistic parents, and often-unsupportive principals. Understandably, in such an environment teachers develop a bunker mentality that encourages them to fight the administration in virtually every situation.

Furthermore, administrators in failing schools know that it will not be easy to replace the unsatisfactory teacher with a better replacement. Parents in these troubled schools offer little support to the administration and leave the administrator with no allies and no support if he or she tries to remove an ineffective teacher. Regrettably, we find that removing the incompetent teacher is most difficult in the very districts with the greatest need for excellent teachers.

The attitude of classroom teachers toward their union is far different than is commonly believed. A realistic estimate is that not more than 5 to 10 percent of teachers have even a modicum of interest in union positions or activities. Few teachers actually ever read their teacher contract. Most teachers look to their administrators and colleagues to help them resolve problems, rather than to their union leadership.

Unfortunately many teachers, like most people, are easily intimidated. In many states teachers are forced to join the union even when they don't wish to. In many contracts, teachers must pay union dues under so-called fair-share provisions in the contract. The rationale for this provision is that all teachers benefit from union negotiations whether or not they belong to the union.

Not surprisingly, the teachers who benefit most from teachers union protections are those who are only marginally competent and would otherwise be required to perform at a higher level or face dismissal. To remove a tenured teacher for cause can cost tens if not hundreds of thousands of dollars and require hundreds of hours of administrative time and effort. This is a major reason school administrators attempt to counsel out poorly performing teachers rather than institute formal dismissal procedures.

Even in school districts with a highly militant teachers union, the number of teachers who are active in union affairs is quite small. Perhaps 98 percent of the teachers belonging to a teachers union never file a single grievance during their teaching career. A grievance is technically an alleged violation of the collective bargaining agreement. Early on it became clear to union leadership that they could not rely on the rank-and-file teacher to initiate the grievance process.

As union leaders of militant unions found it difficult to persuade teachers to file a grievance, even when the leadership thought that the contract had been violated, a new strategy found its way into collective bargaining agreements. This clause enables the union itself to file a grievance even if no specific teacher is willing to do so.

This allows union leaders so inclined to constantly harass and undercut school management while hiding behind the collective of the union, rather than having individual teachers sign their name to a grievance. In some cases grievances are filed over the stated objection of the teacher involved. This gambit is one way that a teachers union can impede the effective operation of a school district. Fortunately, this type of disruptive scenario is played out in relatively few school districts at any given time.

One aspect of militant teachers unions that does cause considerable dissension occurs in states where teacher strikes are legal. The lion's share of the advantages in conflicts between a school board and the local teachers union lies with the teachers. Even if teachers go on strike, state laws require that lost days be made up at the end of the school year. Thus teachers do not ultimately suffer a loss of income in the event of a strike.

Teachers also typically enjoy the goodwill of the parents of their students. School board members can be portrayed as miserly robber barons while the teachers portray themselves as primarily interested in the welfare of students. At the urgings of teachers, parents usually exert strong pressure on their local board members to accede to the demands of the union rather than cause school to be cancelled due to a strike.

In addition to students having their education interrupted, teacher strikes cause considerable disruption in the family lives of the students. In households where both parents work, or in single-parent households, a teacher strike means that students are at home unsupervised when they would otherwise be in school. Teacher strikes significantly interfere with college applications, sports programs, and other services of vital interest to many parents. Strikes also negatively affect student and staff morale long after the strike has been settled.

This alone is a strong incentive for parents to pressure school boards to settle a teacher contract. Typically the 75 percent of taxpayers without students in schools exert little pressure on the school board to control costs during protracted contract negotiations. The complaints of taxpayers most often aren't expressed until the following budget development season when school taxes need to be raised to incorporate the impact of higher labor costs into the school budget.

Taxpayer unrest often expresses itself in the next school board election where board members who have raised taxes are defeated by new board members pledging to control tax increases. The same tax-and-spend scenario then repeats itself so that four to six years later the board turns over once again as a new cadre of tax-resisting board members frequently succumb to the need for new taxes in their turn.

The cost of public education increases inexorably at a rate of inflation plus 2–3 percent per year. The increase over inflation is most often a function of increased staffing for the schools to comply with federal and state mandates, largely in the area of special education. Additional staffing is also necessary to deal adequately with a student population that increasingly requires closer supervision and individual assistance.

As we will see in later chapters, all of the power of teachers unions over the past forty years has not translated into major changes in teachers' salaries relative to the general economy or to other professions. The real financial advantage to teachers over this period has come in the areas of health and pension benefits. Health care benefits for teachers have not been curtailed over the past decade as they have in the private sector.

The benefits themselves are very generous compared with most private plans. The percentage of health care premiums paid by teachers as well as other public employees is very small compared with the share of such costs borne by workers in the private sector. Teachers in many states still enjoy defined benefits pensions that are much more generous than in the private sector. These plans guarantee a lifetime pension based on a formula that generates yearly payments of 60 to 80 percent of the salary earned in the final years of teaching.

Only one-third of Americans, including public employees, currently participate in defined benefits programs. Most Americans, even if they have a pension plan, find themselves in 401(k)-type defined contribution plans rather than defined benefits plans. The pension program for school employees is an immense benefit for the education profession. There is a growing movement in states throughout the nation to scale back pension benefits for teachers and other public employees.

The issue of merit pay is discussed more fully in chapter 5, "The Myth of Merit Pay." For the purpose of this discussion on teachers unions, we need to recognize that a merit-pay system is anathema to any union, including teachers unions. In those few cases where school boards have adamantly insisted on including merit-pay provisions in a teacher contract, the union has managed to undermine the effectiveness of such programs. The contract mechanisms negotiated to assess teacher performance by administrators become so cumbersome that they make the program impractical. Teachers unions have sometimes undermined such merit provisions in very creative ways.

About a decade ago, a suburban Philadelphia school district managed to insert a merit-pay provision in the teacher contract. The intent of the provision was sabotaged by the union by way of securing the agreement of teachers in the district that any awards granted to teachers in terms of merit pay would be donated to a charity. A teacher strike occurred later in the district, and the merit-pay provision was ultimately removed from future contracts.

The downside of collective bargaining agreements as described previously, while regrettable and counterproductive, cannot be claimed as a major factor in preventing needed improvements in the great majority of our public schools. In our largest and poorest performing school districts, however, the influence of the teachers union can be a strong negative for our students. On balance nationally, teachers unions are but a minor obstacle to school improvement when measured against other factors.

In any event, there is little chance that the union genie can be put back in the bottle. Educational policy makers would better expend their energies on supporting efforts to enhance the performance of the existing teacher corps, rather than expect improvements to be made by curbing the influence of teachers unions.

5

The Myth of Merit Pay

Chapter 4 touched upon merit pay as it relates to teachers unions. We saw that unions represent a very staunch and effective opponent to the concept of merit pay. For the sake of discussion, we now assume that teachers unions either do not exist or do not oppose merit pay. Union opposition aside, there are a sufficient number of practical problems with the concept of merit pay to ensure that it never becomes commonplace in schools.

For most of the twentieth century there were recurring intervals when our opinion leaders have jumped on the bandwagon of merit pay as a partial solution to the perceived problems with some of our public schools. Opinion leaders such as the former CEO of IBM, Lou Gestner, became active in promoting merit pay more than a decade ago. Secretary of Education Arne Duncan, former U.S. Speaker of the House Newt Gingrich, and the Reverend Al Sharpton are the most recent high-profile advocates of merit pay. Secretary Duncan initiated a merit-pay plan in some Chicago schools while he was superintendent of schools in Chicago. *Education Week* reports in its June 9, 2010, issue that the program shows no evidence of improved student achievement on math and reading tests compared with a group of similar, nonparticipating schools (Sawchuk, 2010).

There are currently merit-pay plans either operational or in the planning stage in cities such as Houston, Pittsburgh, and Washington, D.C. Perhaps some combination of the newer approaches will be successful and be transferable to other school districts. These enthusiasms generally last for a few years, however, and then quietly fade from the scene—having absolutely no impact on converting the concept of merit pay from theory to practice. Why is this?

Famous business executives, media pundits, and public policy participants are often by nature very competitive people. They assume that most other people are as motivated to compete as they are. This is simply not the case. Teachers are typically motivated both by a desire to make a positive impact on their students and to earn a living for their families. They have no desire for fame, fortune, or status.

Most teachers, as well as people in other helping professions such as nursing, social work, and the clergy, are genuinely offended by the idea that they should compete with one another for merit bonuses or raises. It might be possible to convince teachers to accept the concept of merit pay at the school level, but it will never be accepted at the individual level.

A major difficulty in implementing a valid merit-pay system is the criteria to be used to assess teacher performance. Will standardized test scores be the sole criterion? If so, we are mainly measuring math and reading achievement, subjects that are taught directly for no more than one-third of the school day. How do we assess art and music teachers, guidance counselors, nurses, and other professionals who are critical to the effectiveness of a good school?

Other criteria that would need to be included in a valid teacher evaluation system include the following:

- How the teacher interacts with students in the classroom
- The degree of difficulty of the subject taught
- The nature of the students in the class
- The level of support from the parents
- The overall culture and climate of the school itself

In a typical public school there is one administrator for every twenty teachers. These principals and assistant principals spend most of their time dealing with interpersonal problems involving students, teachers, and parents. A significant portion of their time is spent on the everyday management functions of the school. In most schools the principal finds it difficult to spend even two class periods per year directly observing the performance of each teacher. Such a small sample of actual classroom instruction is not nearly enough to make valid decisions about teacher performance for merit-pay purposes.

Merit-pay proposals seldom consider the resources necessary to successfully implement such a program. We would need to double the administrative resources at each school building to ensure a proper evaluation of each teacher, even if valid standards could be developed. This would be a significant additional cost to implementing a merit-pay program. Many current merit-pay initiatives are financed by foundation grants, deferring the question of the long-term funding to a later date.

On the question of financing a merit-pay system, merit-pay proponents seldom suggest that additional monies ought to be budgeted to implement such a system. Instead, school critics often couple their enthusiasm for merit pay with complaints about the high cost of American education compared with that of other nations. A reasonable inference from the association of these two ideas is that merit-pay proponents are not recommending that we spend more money, but rather that we divert some existing resources from those who are evaluated as less than meritorious to those who are judged as more meritorious.

The implications of this viewpoint are not lost upon the teacher in the trenches. He or she sees this as a plan to increase his or her own income at the expense of the colleague in the next classroom. Or, just as likely, he or she would be the one to receive less compensation in such an essentially zero-sum game.

Such a scenario is not attractive to the typical teacher, whether the merit stipend is worth $1,000 per year or $10,000 per year. If the stipend were $1,000, about $600 after taxes, the thoughtful teacher will conclude that the reward is not worth the negative feelings that would be generated among his less fortunate colleagues who do not receive a merit increase. If the stipends were $10,000 per year, the envy and jealousy engendered in his teacher colleagues would be unacceptable to the meritorious teacher.

Furthermore, a high level of such ill feelings among colleagues would destroy the cohesiveness and collaborative spirit that are essential to a well-functioning school. While the classroom teacher is the single most important school-based factor affecting student performance, he or she is far from the only factor. The general ethos of the school, the quality of the administration, and the efforts of other teachers and support staff each play a role in promoting student achievement.

As the dollar amount at stake in a merit plan increases, the level of internal dissension and dissatisfaction will increase proportionately. Administrators will be accused of favoritism, and teachers will resist unfair comparisons due to the variations of academic ability and interest among different groups of students. There will inevitably be charges of racial, age, and sex discrimination associated with the awards. It is likely that a school district would find itself in litigation over the operations of its merit-pay plan. All of these negative consequences would far outweigh any perceived benefits of a merit-pay system.

Let's review a few of the practical issues that schools would face in trying to implement a merit-pay system. Consider the case of a high school physics teacher who is subject to evaluations based upon the performance of his students on a nationally standardized test in general physics. Physics as a subject is highly dependent upon prior student knowledge of some fairly sophisticated mathematical concepts. Suppose that the math department in this school has not done a good job in teaching these concepts to the students.

How then can the physics teacher be held solely accountable for poor student performance on the national test?

A second example might be a high school teacher of English whose competency will be judged by the performance of her eleventh-grade students on a test of writing skills. These skills are developed over many years and the success or failure of students on a given test cannot be attributed solely to the efforts of the eleventh-grade teacher.

The teacher might be highly effective in improving the skills of a group of ill-prepared students, but the test results might be mediocre at best. Conversely, this teacher could do a poor job of advancing the skill levels of a group of students who already have well-developed skills, but the students would do well on the writing test, falsely indicating that the teacher has done an excellent job.

Finally, consider a fourth-grade teacher in an inner-city elementary school. Many such schools experience a significant turnover in the student body in the course of one year. A few schools experience student turnover exceeding 100 percent. Assume that by the end of the school year this fourth-grade teacher has lost one-half of the students who started the year in her class. To what extent can she be held accountable for the performance of the other half of her students who have replaced half of her original students during the year?

Another danger is that the merit plan, even if implemented, may well be undermined at the operational level. Assume for a moment that a plan exists that provides for $2,000 merit bonuses limited to 10 percent of the faculty of a given school. The school principal, who needs to have a good relationship with all of his staff members on a long-term basis, will be greatly tempted to spread the awards among a large portion of his staff over, say, a five-year period. In this scenario a substantially different group of teachers will be awarded merit bonuses in each of the five years. Thus, over the long term, many if not most teachers will be awarded merit raises or bonuses.

In this scenario a great deal of time and energy would be expended to little positive effect. The merit plan would quickly devolve into an initiative that is all form and no substance. This is a major reason why the few merit-pay plans that have been implemented in public schools are quietly jettisoned after a few years. The earliest references to merit-pay plans for teachers date from the early twentieth century, almost one hundred years ago. This is one school reform proposal that has developed at a truly glacial pace.

Even fairly benign attempts to differentiate among teachers in terms of ratings can easily prove counterproductive. In the 1970s a Pennsylvania school district decided to evaluate teachers on a twenty-point scale, with thirteen points as a passing rating and twenty points indicating teaching excellence. When the high school principal implemented this plan with his one hundred staff members, he noticed a curious phenomenon.

Teachers awarded ratings of 13 or 14 were pleased and relieved that they had not been found unsatisfactory. Teachers who received ratings of 18 or 19 became angry with the principal and insisted on knowing why they had not achieved a rating of 20. The whole exercise produced the opposite of the effect that was intended. The best teachers were disgruntled and the poorer teachers felt complacent and satisfied. Needless to say, this system was eventually scuttled by this school district.

Merit-pay advocates also risk reductionism by assuming that the quality of an educational program can be measured purely in terms of academic achievement in basic academic subjects. How should we answer the question, "What is the purpose of education?" We surely believe that it includes more than performance on tests of basic skills. Good performance in basic skills is a very critical element of a good education, but it does not encompass the entire rationale for publicly supported schools.

A good school teaches a student how to operate effectively in a complex social system. Good teachers provide role models for how to interact with others in a cooperative and productive fashion. This is especially important in a modern society where too many students have few, if any, positive adult role models in their life. Good schools also introduce students to the civic culture of the nation and ultimately prepare the student to participate in our governance.

A good education provides students with lessons in both theoretical and practical morality and ethics. Virtues such as justice, kindness, empathy, perseverance, and honesty are all developed in the context of the day-to-day operation of a good school. Individual teachers contribute to the development of such virtues in ways that cannot be captured by standardized test results.

In measuring the effectiveness or worth of a teacher, how do we capture these ephemeral contributions? No less a hard-core scientist than Albert Einstein once said, "Not everything that counts can be counted, and not everything that can be counted, counts." The lesson is that we need to be careful that we don't reduce the essence of education only to that which can be easily measured.

Evaluating schools and teachers exclusively on what can be measured will tend to divert our attention from other factors that are essential to the full development of the next generation of Americans. Conversely, if we attempt to develop an evaluation model that takes the more ephemeral and less quantitative factors into consideration, we will create an overly complex and controversial model.

Such a model would be dependent upon subjective judgments by supervisors that would fail to gain acceptance among teachers. Creating such a complex model that would be both valid and reliable would prove impossible, and unaffordable even if such a model could be developed.

An interesting irony is that the strongest advocates of merit pay for teachers, with student academic achievement as the sole criterion for excellence, are generally people of a conservative philosophical bent who also trumpet the importance of values education. They seem to assume a necessary correlation between good academic performance and good values. A look at the despicable and unethical behavior of many of the best and the brightest on Wall Street in recent years should disabuse us of any necessary correlation between academic achievement and ethical behavior.

Descending from the Olympian heights from which the punditocracy discusses educational issues, let's look at teaching from the point of view of the teacher. What are the day-to-day constraints that affect the quality of instruction in a given classroom? More than most endeavors, teaching and learning are greatly influenced by the state of mind of both the instructor and the students.

Students can be easily distracted by a host of issues ranging from breaking up with a girlfriend or boyfriend to economic and interpersonal stressors within the family unit. In today's world social networking mechanisms such as Facebook, cell phones, and text messaging are major distractions for students. The effectiveness of the teacher, too, more so than a line worker in a tire plant, for example, is affected by her state of mind and distractions from her personal life.

This dynamic affects the classroom climate by the extent to which students are negatively affected by personal and family problems, economic and social stress, or mental or physical disabilities that may affect learning. All of theses negative factors are more prominent in dysfunctional socioeconomic neighborhoods than in more stable middle-class families and communities. Teachers in such challenging environments are at a considerable disadvantage in helping their students to perform at the same level as students from more favored backgrounds.

Even within a given school, the extent to which different groups of students can affect the learning environment in a classroom is surprising. Anyone with even a modicum of teaching experience will acknowledge that the mix of personalities in each group of students gives each class a particular chemistry. If the chemistry skews to the negative side, students in that class will not perform as well as students in a class with a more positive chemistry or tone.

Thus the same teacher may be more successful in teaching the second-period geometry class than the fourth-period geometry class—same teacher, same subject, and same lesson preparation, but with a different mix of students. To some extent, the academic performance of a given class in a given year is influenced by the luck of the draw. Any primary school teacher will tell you that her group of twenty-five students can differ greatly from one year to the next in both academic interest and ability.

A classroom teacher is significantly affected by the general ethos of the school itself. A teacher in a school with a weak principal, where student discipline is poor, and where his or her teaching colleagues are mediocre or dispirited will not be as effective as he or she would be in more benign circumstances. A more global influence on the effectiveness of this teacher is the culture of the general community in which he or she finds himself or herself.

If parents do not support the school or their child, and if the general attitude of other students is antiacademic, the teacher will be far less effective than otherwise. This type of negative school ethos is all too common in many schools of our inner cities and cannot be easily ameliorated by new evaluation models such as merit pay.

In spite of the difficulties faced by many inner-city schools, there are always teachers and principals who produce excellent results by dint of a strong personality and sheer determination. These exceptional educators cannot be mass-produced, however, and overall school success requires that schools be created wherein ordinary mortals can produce exceptional results.

In chapter 18, "International Comparisons," we compare American schools to those in other developed nations. One area of comparison is the extent to which schools in other countries incorporate merit-pay plans into their systems. We will see that merit pay is not a general practice in the very school systems that our public school critics point to as worthy of emulation.

Turning to the business world, we find that ambitious merit-pay schemes do not always correlate with the best performing businesses. One company, for example, aggressively recruited the best graduates from business schools, rewarded their top performers handsomely, and relentlessly weeded out employees rated poorly. The company was Enron.

Another company, Southwest Airlines, is recognized as among the best performing airlines. Southwest pays its managers modestly. It awards raises according to seniority rather than the "rank and yank" system employed by Enron. It enjoys a stellar reputation for customer satisfaction and employee loyalty and performance (Gladwell, 2009, 357–373). Southwest is now the most successful domestic airline in the United States.

The lesson to be learned from these two cases is not that merit-pay systems never work, or that a time-in-grade compensation plan is necessarily superior. Rather, the point is that merit-pay plans are not a magic bullet that guarantees organizational success, nor is a time-in-grade compensation plan inimical to good organizational performance.

Merit-pay plans are not an effective incentive for the great majority of teachers, but would merely serve as a further dispiriting element in the school environment. In a merit-pay environment, we may well lose some teachers who at least are willing to make a valiant attempt to teach in difficult environments.

We may actually exacerbate the current serious problem of attracting good teachers to underperforming schools.

Chapter 19, "Final Exam," offers recommendations for modifying the salary schedule to attract more young people to teaching and to attract teachers at every career stage to offer their services to our urban school districts. If the time and energy needed to implement a merit-pay system were invested in improving the climate and practices in the schools, themselves, we would bring about some significant improvement in our underperforming schools.

6

School Charters, Vouchers, and Privatization

The concepts of charter schools, vouchers, and privatization as solutions to the problems of public education owe their intellectual genesis to the works of Milton Friedman in *Free to Choose* (1980) and Chubb and Moe in *Politics, Markets and America's Schools* (1990). The Chubb and Moe book was a direct result of the perceived failure of the public school reforms of the 1980s following the *A Nation at Risk* Department of Education study of 1983.

That study generated reform efforts including higher graduation requirements, high-stakes testing at the state level, and effort to improve the education and practice of classroom teachers. By 1990 these efforts had produced only minimal improvements. The thrust of reform efforts eventually shifted to the federal level, culminating in the No Child Left Behind Act in 2001.

The major concept behind the school charter and privatization movements is that by releasing competitive forces in public education, the monopoly of the public schools would be broken. This would lead to better school performance through parents choosing to send their children to the best-performing schools, thereby forcing public schools to either improve or wither on the vine.

The charter movement also gave rise to the privatization initiative, best exemplified by the Edison Project created by Christopher Whittle. This effort was based on the notion that not only could Edison-operated schools lead to better student performance, but that they could do so at a profit to investors. The more traditional charter school movement, however, was based on the theory that such schools would simply perform better than public schools without concern for profitability. Each state developed its own charter school law, so regulations vary somewhat from state to state. There are, however, certain common features among charter schools across the nation.

Charter schools are usually funded at the same level as the instructional cost per pupil in the local public school district. Charters are awarded either by the local district or the state, and such schools are subject to the same state testing requirements as regular public schools. These schools cannot be operated by religious institutions and must be neutral regarding religion, as are public schools.

Charter schools cannot discriminate among students for admission and teachers must have state certification similar to that of public school teachers. Some states require certification for only a high percentage of charter teachers rather than for all teachers, as in public schools. Teachers in charter schools must also participate in the state teachers' retirement system. Unions are typically not found in charter schools—a fact that is considered beneficial to the schools. Charter schools often feature longer school days and a longer school year than regular public schools. This is a major advantage for many parents, especially working parents.

The Knowledge is Power Program (KIPP) group of charter schools, for example, features school days running from 7:30 a.m. to 5:00 p.m., with four hours of school on Saturdays. The schools have a two-hundred-day school year. In contrast, the neighboring public schools in cities with KIPP charter schools usually operate from 8:30 a.m. to 3:00 p.m. with no Saturday school. The school year in a typical public school is 180 days. We will shortly explore how these charter schools are able to offer almost 50 percent more instructional time for students with the same per-pupil budget as the public schools in their communities.

KIPP schools are not without their critics. Some critics say that KIPP schools have a high attrition rate, usually among students who do not adhere to its rigorous standards. Other critics claim that the admissions process self-screens for students who are highly motivated and compliant. Without vouching for the validity of these criticisms, they are reasonable assertions that need to be considered.

Country Day in Harlem operates in a manner quite similar to the KIPP charter schools (Davidson, 2009, 70). This model differs from most public charter schools, however, in that it is a private school with tuition between $400 and $16,000 per year, depending upon financial ability.

The headmaster, Vincent Dotoli, states that the school accepts only one in four applicants. He freely acknowledges that only students with highly motivated parents are admitted. All parents must donate four hours per month to work for the school. Each class has two teachers and no more than sixteen students. School revenues are heavily subsidized by grants sponsored by J. P. Morgan and Goldman Sachs. Dotoli credits much of the success of the school to motivated parents. He points out, however, that his students are no wealthier, on average, than other students in Harlem.

The selection of students for charter schools cannot be discriminatory in any way. Most schools employ a lottery system since there are frequently more applicants than available slots. To say that students are chosen by lottery is not to say that selection is random. Selection is from among the students of parents who formally apply to send their children to these schools.

Thus to compare the performance of students in charter schools to students in regular public schools is not statistically valid. Charter school students come from homes where the parents sufficiently value education to seek a better school for their children. This is not the case for many of the parents of the students in nearby public schools. This important distinction is frequently overlooked when comparing student performance in regular public schools to student performance in charter schools.

A more rigorous study in New York City, reported in *The Wall Street Journal* of September 22, 2009, compared charter school students to students who had applied but not been admitted to the charter schools through the lottery system. After eight years in the charter school students scored 680 on a mathematics test while their public school counterparts who had applied for, but not been accepted for the charter schools, scored 650 on the same test (Hechinger and Dugan, 2009). A score of 650 is considered proficient on this test.

The score differential does not seem dramatic given that the non–charter school students continued to deal with the milieu and peer pressures of the regular public school, did not have longer school days or school years, and did not have lower class sizes as in the charter school. Furthermore, charter schools typically have high attrition rates for students who cannot adapt to the discipline standards or the rigorous academic regimen. Students who have been in the charter school for eight years are certainly among the most motivated and well disciplined of the cohort that started at the school eight years before.

This study follows a more defensible sample selection procedure than most studies, but still has one critical defect. The charter school and public school students in the study both came from homes where parents had taken the initiative to have their student apply for entrance to a charter school. In neither instance are we talking about the typical student in a dysfunctional school and community. Given the similar scores for both groups, the study serves to reinforce the theory that interested and motivated parents are the key to student achievement.

The fairest test of the efficacy of charter schools would be to randomly assign students from a given disadvantaged neighborhood to charter schools or to regular public schools. Such a study would most likely show little or no difference in achievement for public versus charter school students. The charter schools would then grapple with the same challenge as nearby public schools—a large percentage of parents who are not attentive to their children's education.

By the late 1990s most states had operating charter schools generally following the model described previously. How have these schools fared over the past decade both in terms of student performance and in the proportion of parents who send their children to such schools? The most salient fact is that the charter school movement is concentrated in urban school districts where the regular public schools are the least successful.

After twenty years of the charter school movement, about 3 percent of public school children attend charter schools. There are approximately four thousand charter schools distributed among the forty or so states that allow them. As of 2004, about 55 percent of charter school students were black or Hispanic and attended charter schools in economically disadvantaged parts of our large cities. About 45 percent of children attending charter schools nationwide were white (Snyder, Dillow, and Hoffman, 2009, 161–162).

A National Assessment of Educational Progress study in 2003 comparing student achievement in charter schools and matched public schools found little difference in student performance in charter schools versus comparable public schools. Over time, the argument for charter schools has changed from the assertion that competition would lead to better student performance to the issue of equity. The currently favored rational is that parents should have the right to transfer their students from failing public schools to charter schools that might better meet their children's needs.

Two suburban Philadelphia public school systems that differ greatly in the proportion of students attending charter schools varied dramatically. One school community with a high proportion of disadvantaged children enrolled almost 20 percent of its potential student body in nearby charter schools. The other extremely affluent school district in the Philadelphia suburbs enrolled only 3 of its 3,600 students in charter schools. A fairly high proportion of students in this affluent district attended private schools. Parents who chose the public schools, however, had no interest in choosing the charter school option.

Parents who choose charter schools are generally pleased with their choice. This is also true, in general, for parents of students in private and parochial schools. The dynamic at play here may be nothing more than the normal proclivity of people to express satisfaction with choices they have made for themselves, whether it be a choice of a spouse, a car, a neighborhood, or a home. This may explain why parents rate the schools that their children actually attend higher than they rate public schools in general.

Public schools, on the other hand, suffer the same disadvantage as the post office and the department of motor vehicles. They are the default option provided by the government. Parents in many cases do not so much choose their schools, but simply send their children to the local school to which they have been assigned. In this scenario parents have no special commitment to their school as compared with parents who have actively selected a school for their children.

The data on charter school attendance beg the question as to why a larger proportion of parents have not chosen to send their children to charter schools. Regrettably, the tepid response to the charter school option in many of our dysfunctional communities often reflects a lack of sufficient concern and interest on the part of parents. The good news is that some parents who are committed to better schools for their children now have options other than a failing public school.

Charter schools are limited in suburban and rural areas either because people are basically satisfied with their public schools or because the geographic distances and implications for busing are such that charter schools are simply impractical to operate. The development of virtual or cyber charter schools may resolve the geographic and busing issues in more rural areas. In any event, charter schools have not brought about the revolutionary change in public schooling that their early proponents expected.

Groups of interested parents as well as community action groups interested in education have founded most existing charter schools. Entrepreneurs, whose motivations include personal gain and increasing shareholders' value, have founded a significant minority of charter schools. As reported in the *Philadelphia Inquirer* of August 16, 2009, at least five charter schools in Philadelphia are being investigated by federal authorities for financial malfeasance (Woodall and Shiffman, 2009, B01). Another *Philadelphia Inquirer* article on October 23, 2009, reported that the CEO of the Philadelphia Academy Charter School had been sentenced to three years in federal prison for stealing funds from the school (Woodall, 2009, A01).

Charter school students bring the same per-pupil expenditure to the school as public schools receive for their students. There are additional services provided to charter schools by the public school system such as busing and nursing services. Charter schools also have the ability to raise funds independently of the school district. In too many cases an unjustified proportion of available funds at charter schools are being spent to overcompensate the school's management. The proportion of charter schools involved in financial malfeasance is certainly small, but it appears to be greater than the proportion of such skullduggery in the public schools.

One of the heralded benefits of charter schools is that they are not subject to all of the bureaucracy and regulations of regular public schools. The downside of this loose regulatory regimen is that unprincipled management has greater opportunities to finesse the system for its own benefit, rather than that of the children or staff.

The original proponents of charter school believed that the entrepreneurial spirit of the business world would be easily transferrable to the education world. Those who have worked in social service organizations such as
schools, hospitals, and similar enterprises, however, can attest that the typical
employee in these organizations has little interest in competing with other
similar entities. The average nurse or teacher is interested in performing a
vital service to others and in being compensated reasonably. Managers of
charter schools who are entrepreneurial and competitive find it difficult to
transfer their passion for competition to their frontline employees.

Teachers can be motivated to improve for the sake of their students and
better academic performance, but not to operate more efficiently for the sake
of improving the bottom line. Those who attempt to implement merit-pay
plans confront this reality repeatedly and find that teachers are not interested
in competition even if it can personally benefit them in terms of additional
compensation.

In examining the financing of charter schools, several questions come to
mind. If we assume that per-pupil expenditures closely match those in regular public schools, how is it possible for charter schools to offer additional
services such as a longer school day and longer school year? How can many
management personnel in some charter schools be compensated at a level
significantly above comparable public school administrators?

There is often a cap on class sizes that allow charter schools to staff more
efficiently than in typical public schools. If a charter school decides to cap
second-grade class size at twenty-five and has six teachers, no more than 150
students will be admitted as second graders. A public school district, on the
other hand, might have 150 second-grade students distributed among three
small elementary schools.

Assume that the public school also decides to cap class sizes at twenty-five.
Because there are eighty students in one school, four teachers will be needed.
There may be thirty-five students in each of the other two elementary schools
requiring two teachers in each school. Thus the public school will need eight
teachers rather than six—a 33 percent increase in staffing needs compared
with a charter school with the same class-size standard.

In these situations public schools sometimes reassign students to another
school, increasing busing costs and upsetting the parents involved. Another
option is to allow class sizes to rise to twenty-seven in the largest school and
to thirty-five in the other two schools. Both parents and teachers strongly resist this option. The charter school, with a cap on admissions, does not have
these endemic inefficiencies that raise costs in the public schools.

The absolute cap on class size in charter schools promotes a higher level
of both parental satisfaction and operational efficiency. While public schools

must admit any student in its attendance area, charter schools where class size limits have been met will only admit new students as vacancies occur in their classes.

Teachers in both public schools and charter schools are compensated on a salary scale that financially rewards teachers according to years of experience. A typical public school system may have average teacher tenure of thirteen to fifteen years. The average experience level of teachers in charter schools, at least in these early years, may be only three to four years. This makes a significant difference in salary and benefit costs for charter versus regular public schools. Also, charter schools often have a high level of teacher attrition, keeping the average experience level, and thus salaries, lower than they otherwise would be.

Another factor that lowers the average experience level of teachers in charter schools is the movement of these teachers to regular public schools. Regular public school positions are favored by many teachers in charter schools because of their perceived greater job security and higher pay as teachers gain more experience. The typical time commitment for a regular public school teacher also tends to be less than that of a teacher in a charter school.

For young female teachers who envision raising children in their future, a position with a more mother-friendly school schedule is very attractive. The human resources department in one public school district received many applications from teachers in nearby charter schools. Few if any teachers from the public school district applied for positions in the charter schools.

An interesting dynamic occurred at a symposium on educational issues held many years ago that was sponsored by a prestigious private school in the Philadelphia suburbs. The public school superintendent at the meeting found himself surrounded at his lunch table by young teachers at this private high school. All of these teachers were asking how to go about being hired by a public school. These young teachers were not expressing dissatisfaction with their current positions, but were merely reacting as most people would to the higher salaries and greater job security available as public school teachers.

Two other financial advantages for charter schools over public schools are a function of the relative youth and lower salary of the teaching staff mentioned previously. In Pennsylvania, charter school teachers are a part of the public school pension program. A charter school's required pension contributions are far less than in a public school, however, because contributions are based on the salaries of the generally less-experienced and lower-paid teachers in the charter school.

The youthful teaching corps in charter schools also positively affects premium costs for group health insurance in charter schools versus regular public schools. A younger and healthier group of teachers will have a positive effect on health insurance premiums for these schools. If the average experience level of charter school teachers increases over the years, personnel costs will rise and charter schools will not be able to offer extended-day and extended-year services within the budgetary allocations dictated by public school per-pupil expenditures.

Milton Friedman's advocacy of school vouchers reached fruition in 1990 in the city of Milwaukee. This program was fairly successful and led to an expansion of the concept to eighteen sites in ten states and the District of Columbia (Goodman, 2009, 8). The Washington, D.C., program, while very popular, was discontinued by the Obama administration. There are currently about 170,000 students in voucher programs nationwide. These data indicate a very slow level of adaptation of this concept over the past twenty years. Many comparisons of student achievement in voucher programs versus public schools throughout this period have been ambiguous at best.

A discussion of the fate of the Edison Project offers a fitting end to this chapter. In 1991 entrepreneur Chris Whittle formed a for-profit corporation to make schooling profitable for investors while at the same time competing with existing public schools to improve student performance. Conservative think tanks such as the Heritage Foundation as well as the conservative *Wall Street Journal* hailed the new initiative. Conservative thinkers such as Chester Finn and John Chubb were instrumental in the creation of this new project.

Whittle's vision was to operate one thousand for-profit schools over the following decade. Hundreds of millions of dollars were raised to fund the project. The organization traded on NASDAQ for a four-year period in the late 1990s, with the stock trading as high as $40 a share in early 2001. Thereafter the share price tumbled to $0.14 per share. The company was taken private in 2003 through a buyout that paid only $1.75 per share (Parents Advocating School Accountability, 2009).

The company changed its model before long to one that would contract to operate public schools, mainly in the big cities, rather than operate its own private schools. Virtually all of these contracts eventually lapsed since student performance did not exceed that of comparable public schools, and in many cases student performance was inferior. The organization morphed into a supplemental tutoring model in recent years and at present Mr. Whittle is trying to begin a new venture in founding high-end private schools.

The Edison Project was heralded in the early 1990s as the way of the future for privatization of schooling, but its ultimate failure has gone virtually unremarked in the media. What came in with a bang in 1991 went out with a whimper in 2008. School privatization has failed to be a widespread alternative to public education. Charter schools have been more successful as a niche market in some communities with dysfunctional schools. Voucher programs have had a few scattered successes but ultimately haven't been able to overcome the American aversion to public funds for private schools.

We will revisit the charter school topic in chapter 19, "Final Exam." There we will explore examples of charter schools that appear to be particularly successful. Ultimately, however, the charter school movement will be seen as a faulty model for improving education on a large scale.

7

The Legal Tangle in Education

The intrusion of the legal system into every element of public education has been a major factor in the increased cost and complexity in the schools over the past forty years. Since the 1960s the legal system has greatly impacted relationships between students and teachers and between teachers and parents, as well as between school administrators and parents. The complexities of this legal tangle have forced school administrators and school boards to rely heavily on the legal advice of their school district solicitors.

Let us first consider the radically changed relationship between students and teachers since the 1960s. Back in the 1960s the traditional legal interpretation of the rights of school officials vis-à-vis students, known as in loco parentis, was still the norm in most states and school districts. This legal principle held that during the school day teachers and administrators stood in a parental relationship with students.

This meant that for practical purposes, the teachers had authority over students similar to that exercised by the students' parents. This gave teachers and principals great latitude in their ability to impose good discipline over students and to expect ready compliance from students to staff directives and requests.

The social turmoil of the late 1960s soon spilled over into the schools. The younger brothers and sisters of the Vietnam War protesters and draft protesters began to imitate their older siblings by bringing protests into the public schools, often manifested as large-scale walkouts and other disruptive activities by students. This was the heyday of sit-down strikes, streakers running through the halls naked, and pot smoking in student restrooms.

Supreme Court cases such as *Tinker vs. Des Moines* gave students the legal right to wear armbands protesting the Vietnam War or express other signs of dissidence in the school, so long as such protests did not create substantive disruption to the educational process. The onus of proving substantial disruption was placed on the school. Whereas formerly school officials could use their own professional judgments as to what constitutes a disruptive activity, they now had to be prepared to defend their actions in court. Parents began to challenge school officials in court, often through suits initiated by the American Civil Liberties Union.

By the early 1970s many states had developed legislation often referred to as *Student Rights and Responsibilities.* Such legislation required school administrators to follow a quasilegal framework for making decisions on student discipline that had previously been considered solely within the purview of school officials. These new regulations limited disciplinary action toward a disruptive student to a verbal reprimand, assignment to an after-school detention, or perhaps an in-school suspension. Removing the student from the school for extended periods became quite difficult and in some districts virtually impossible.

The school principal could be subjected to a lawsuit that would be costly to the school district and consume substantial amounts of the administrator's time and energy. Losing such a court case could seriously damage the administrator's career and would cause him to lose face and respect within the school community. Not surprisingly, the level of good discipline in many schools suffered as administrators became more wary of potential legal problems arising from student disciplinary encounters.

The quasilegal procedures now mandated to process even relatively minor disciplinary infractions required more administrative time and placed greater burdens on the classroom teacher as well. Before sending a student to the office for a disciplinary infraction, the teacher now needed to fill out a disciplinary form describing the infraction in detail. These forms eventually took on the formality of police incidence reports.

Under the new rules of evidence, administrators needed to allow the accused student to confront any student witnesses to the infraction. This made it far more difficult to prove the guilt of the student. Many potential student witnesses refused to confront the accused student out of fear of retribution from the student at a later time—after school, over the weekend, or even the following summer.

Parents understandably began to resist having their own children involved in the disciplinary process involving another student. It became far more difficult to enforce a healthy level of discipline in the schools, particularly with middle and high school–aged students. Teachers naturally sought to avoid the paperwork and potential confrontation with students or their parents inherent in making disciplinary referrals. Thus, for many teachers, the standard of acceptable behavior in classrooms slowly began to deteriorate.

The same onerous paperwork requirements and the possibility of confrontations with parents and students also applied to student misbehavior in the halls, the cafeteria, and on the playground. Again, teachers naturally tried to avoid such negative situations by closing the classroom door and avoiding involvement outside their own classrooms. This contributed to more disruptive behavior in these general areas of the school, leading to more disciplinary incidents to be resolved by the now-overburdened school administrators.

Over the years this trend of requiring educators to adhere closely to cumbersome procedures to properly discipline students generated a need for more administrative and clerical support. Such additional assistance was needed to process the procedures required by the new rules. Additional professionals such as extra guidance counselors, social workers, and even psychologists found their way into the schools to counsel students into better behavioral patterns. The ratio of such support personnel to teachers increased quickly as more and more support personnel were needed to maintain a businesslike environment in the schools. The magnitude of the number of new support personnel required will be detailed in chapter 16, "School Finance."

The general level of good discipline in the schools today has deteriorated somewhat compared with forty years ago. An argument can be made, however, that the more therapeutic approach to student misbehavior found in today's schools works fairly well. The downside is that the cost of operating the schools has increased significantly in order to fund the additional administrators, counselors, and mental health professionals now commonplace in the schools.

The modern approach to student discipline places greater pressures on educators as they try to perform an increasingly difficult job. This pressure is particularly intense among school administrators. The number of teachers seeking school administrative jobs has decreased markedly over the past forty years. This is despite the fact that we have many more women pursuing administrative certification today, whereas forty years ago virtually all school administrators were men.

Although we have a potential pool of administrative candidates that has more than doubled, the number of applicants for available administrative positions has declined dramatically. In the 1960s and 1970s, for example, there might have been fifty or more candidates for a school superintendent's position. Today, in these same districts, a superintendent's position may attract as few as ten applicants. A similarly small pool of candidates applies across the board for all administrative positions from assistant principals to principals to central office administrators.

Another legal impact on the schools concerns the relationship between parents and the schools. We are a much more litigious society than we were forty years ago, and this impulse to sue has arrived at the schoolhouse door. Today's parents attended school in the 1980s and 1990s, a time when increased student rights both in discipline and academics had already been fully imbedded into the operation of the schools.

Today's parents are very comfortable in taking a legalistic approach to contentious issues involving their students. The evolution of special education law, described later in this chapter, has also contributed to this more legalistic perspective by the general population of students and parents.

The first major piece of federal special education law, the Education of All Handicapped Act of 1975, greatly expanded the rights of parents of special education students vis-à-vis their local school district. Students now had the right to an Individualized Education Program (IEP), designed by school personnel but requiring the approval of the parents before it could be implemented.

Parents who did not agree with a proposed IEP could challenge the school district's proposal through an appeal process that might ultimately need to be adjudicated by state-appointed hearing officers. Parents had the right to be represented by counsel. School districts responded to this escalation by retaining their own special education counsel to argue the school district's side of the issue.

The merits of a particular case aside, districts now had an incentive to accede to parental demands rather than incur the costs and aggravation of formal special education hearings. Districts now had to employ a cost-benefit analysis to determine whether it would be more costly to pursue the special education hearing or agree to the parental demand that could well be more costly than the hearing. Over the years legal precedents greatly expanded the rights of parents under the law and greatly complicated the job of special education personnel in performing their special education function. In today's world each such special education hearing can cost a school district $30,000 or more.

In the past decade or two parents have been able to secure full-time aides to accompany seriously handicapped students throughout the school day to assist students with compensating for severe physical, emotional, or learning problems. Even so, some of these seriously disabled students have great difficulty participating in the activities of a regular classroom. The inclusion of these students in regular education programs is necessary to fulfill the "least restrictive environment" requirements of federal special education laws.

Salary and benefits for each of these full-time aides can exceed $30,000 to $40,000 a year. Even a rather small school district of three thousand students may need to invest hundreds of thousands of dollars each year to provide one-on-one aides. Large school districts spend millions of dollars on this one service.

In recent years an increasing number of parents have pursued the special education hearing route not simply to object to the plan offered by the public school, but to demand a private-school placement for the student. Such demands are based on the argument that the public schools cannot adequately provide for the special needs of the particular student. Once the hearing officer agrees with the parents and mandates a private-school placement, the school district then assumes a tuition obligation of $50,000 to $100,000 or more a year for that student.

In recent years an entire legal niche has developed for lawyers specializing in special education law. These lawyers advise parent on the latest strategies to optimize the level of school-district support for their student. In addition, a cadre of special education advocates has evolved who advise parents on their rights under the law. These advocates often attend meetings between administrators and parents to advise parents and press the school district for additional services.

The success of special education parents in gaining special advantages for their students has not been lost on parents of regular education students. Some parents have tried to have their children identified as special education students simply to provide them with access to special services. Parents who have a child in special education often approach the educational programs for their regular education students with the same assertiveness that they bring to special education discussions.

Parents in many communities have formed special education parents groups. These groups exist to maximize the services provided to their special education students. Thus many districts now have a powerful pressure group dedicated to achieving new or higher levels of student services. Parents of students identified as gifted are also eligible for special education services, and they can be among the most demanding of pressure groups. In districts with tightly constrained budgets, these services can only come from services that would otherwise be provided to the general student body, whose parents are not so well organized.

The impulse of parents to threaten a lawsuit makes it necessary for teachers and administrators to practice "defensive education." This is very similar to the scenario of defensive medicine that proves so costly to our medical system. The same dynamic is at work in the field of education, although presently not to the same degree as in medicine. Teachers and administrators, confronted by increasingly demanding parents, must invest greater amounts of time and energy developing legally impregnable programs for both regular and special education students.

This is not to say that parents should supinely accept whatever the school recommends. Nonetheless, unreasonable demands by parents add to educational costs and exert additional pressure on already overburdened schoolteachers and officials.

School officials are often threatened with lawsuits on a regular basis. In some districts there seem to be several lawsuits each month; in other districts there is a lawsuit, or threat thereof, at least monthly. Thirty or forty years ago in most public school districts, years passed without the threat of a lawsuit. The potential for legal action makes teachers, principals, and central-office personnel far more tentative in following their professional judgments than would otherwise be the case.

The financial impact of state and federal special education laws at the local school district level is dramatic. Over recent decades the U.S. Congress has mandated an expanding series of new rights for students with disabilities. Originally, the federal government agreed to assume about one-third of the cost of implementing the new legal obligations. States and local districts were expected to share the remaining two-thirds of the program cost. The federal government quickly reneged on its pledge to pay one-third of the rapidly burgeoning costs.

Through the 1980s most states assumed a large share of the growing burden shifted from the federal government. By the 1990s most states made changes in state reimbursements designed to shift a growing proportion of special education costs to local school districts. By the first decade of this century, local districts found themselves bearing an ever-greater portion of costs brought about by legislation at both the state and federal levels. This scenario is a problem for local school districts throughout the nation.

The No Child Left Behind Act of 2001 is a recent example of federal laws having a major financial impact on state and local education budgets. This act requires an increase in state testing as well as remediation programs designed to improve schools found deficient under the testing program.

While federal funding has increased to partially offset the cost of testing and remediation, districts with the least ability to pay soon found themselves engaging in rather expansive remediation programs. These less wealthy districts are often the districts with the largest number of students requiring remediation. Such programs involve the hiring of additional personnel, which is only partially offset by federal or state funds.

This law appears to have had some degree of success. The level of success is debatable, however, since individual states establish the standards of acceptable student performance for their state. This creates dramatically different standards among the states—often changing from year to year to meet political and funding constraints in a given state. Many states have shown impressive gains in student performance over the past eight years according to their own state testing standards.

Unfortunately, much of the improvement can be attributed to massaging the data at the state level. The National Assessment of Educational Progress, a federal test given to a sampling of America's students, shows much more modest gains in recent years compared with data generated by the states. A substantial price has been paid in recent years for the meager gains reflected in national testing data.

The growing complexity of special education law has created reluctance among administrative personnel throughout the school hierarchy to act confidently based on their professional training and experience. In many school districts today we find that principals and assistant principals are calling school district solicitors directly for legal advice. These conversations have typically involved questions about proper legal procedures on student-discipline and staff-supervision issues.

School district lawyers were happy to accommodate such questions and charged accordingly at their hourly rates of $150 an hour or more. District office administrators from special education, human resources, and the business department were also requesting legal counsel far too frequently. Districts that fail to control these excessive contacts between administrators and lawyers experience a far higher level of legal fees than they otherwise would.

Thirty years ago a semirural school district with perhaps 2,500 students might experience annual legal costs of $1,200. This retainer was based on a $100-per-meeting stipend for the solicitor to attend the monthly school board meetings. Twenty-five years later at the school district immediately adjacent to this semirural school district, the annual legal fees were approaching $600,000. Granted that the district was three times larger, the legal landscape had changed significantly, and the community itself was more litigious.

Nevertheless, this enormous increase in legal fees is beyond reason and reflects changing legal requirements and practices in the schools. In recent years in an affluent school district of 3,600 students, annual legal fees ranged between $300,000 and $400,000. This transpired in a district where the school board itself had three lawyers as members.

The major categories of legal challenges to school districts in recent years are labor relations issues, special education challenges, and parental lawsuits relating to student disciplinary or academic issues. Many school districts in states that require collective bargaining for school employees generally hire legal counsel to directly negotiate with the representatives of the various unions. The legal involvement in schools has reached the point where even relatively small school districts must consider full-time district-employed legal counsel to meet the demand for legal representation.

In heavily unionized states many school boards are required to negotiate with five to seven different employee unions. The school board may be negotiating with two or three of these unions at any given time. Aside from the teachers union, most districts in union-friendly states also have unions for food service workers, custodial and maintenance personnel, bus drivers, and support staff personnel, as well as meet-and-discuss requirements for administrative personnel. Even central-office administrators now have individual contracts that require review and negotiations with lawyers representing the interests of the school district.

Most unionized states have required public employee negotiations for thirty-five years or more. In recent decades there are typically very few changes in contracts from one contract period to the next. Most serious contractual issues have been long-since resolved and incorporated into contract language. Nonetheless, there are many useless negotiations sessions where the only beneficiaries are the lawyers, who do not mind long, drawn-out negotiations billed at $150–$200 an hour.

In one district, however, negotiations with the support union had been going on for close to a year with virtually no progress being made. Once the administration entered directly into these negotiations without legal counsel, the contract was settled in a few hours. This intervention required no magic, but simply cut to the essentials and avoided much of the nitpicking that the district's legal firm had a vested interest in pursuing. Similar negotiation stalemates occur with various unions throughout the nation that can sometimes be resolved in a similar manner with less cost for professional negotiators.

There are now court-mandated legal requirements, known as Loudermill hearings, which afford all school employees the right to a dismissal hearing with school district personnel even in the most blatant cases of employee misbehavior. These protections are in addition to any job protection provisions that might be contained in a collective bargaining agreement or state law.

Such employee hearings are required even in egregious cases, such as an employee assaulting another employee or where an employee makes sexual advances toward special education students. In formal legal settings such as Loudermill hearings the district needs to be represented by legal counsel. Each of these hearings can cost a district several thousand dollars.

In one district there was a female custodian who repeatedly filed sexual harassment charges against her coworkers and supervisors. There was little likelihood that the allegations were valid, but of course the allegations needed to be thoroughly investigated. This recurring scenario mercifully came to an end when police arrested the woman for running naked through a local public park. Even in our litigious environment, everyone recognizes that a woman this unstable should not be working in our schools.

The processing of grievances that are filed under the various labor contracts represents another drain on school district resources. Here again legal counsel is usually required to research relevant law and legal decisions pertinent to a given issue. Several thousand dollars can be expended on each grievance filed. In districts with very aggressive or confrontational unions, the number of grievances filed each year can generate a significant cost in legal fees. Many contracts today allow a grievance to be filed by the union itself on a particular issue, even if the person or persons directly affected do not wish to file a grievance.

The impact of special education law on legal fees has been addressed previously. There is also a subtle impact of special education laws in terms of state regulations and their interpretation. States interpret the federal laws and court decisions into guidelines for implementing the laws in the schools.

Such guidelines deal with maximum caseloads for various types of disabilities as well as the certification requirements for staff members working with identified special education students. Parents and the teaching staff both tend to pressure school authorities to interpret these guidelines as liberally as possible. Such pressures maximize services provided to students and encourage generous staffing levels to implement such services.

There is no countervailing force to conserve district financial or human resources. Over time these realities increase the costs of special education programs and lead either to an overall increase in school costs or to the diversion of resources from regular education to special education. Such diversions of scarce resources, often the result of political pressure from interest groups, lead to decisions based on political pressures rather than strictly educational rationales as determined by the educational professionals.

The influence of the legal system on public education has had dramatic effects over the past forty years. In terms of school financing, legal requirements have led to ballooning costs for legal advice. Less visible are the extra manpower costs, mainly for administrative personnel, necessary to provide the special educations safeguards and student disciplinary procedures required to implement legal mandates. Perhaps as much as 20 percent of the increased cost of education over this period can be attributed, either directly or indirectly, to the legal pressures on the schools.

The role of the legal system in education has unquestionably led to genuine reforms and advances. It is equally true, however, that the degree of legal involvement in the schools has added to the bureaucracy, diminished the role of educational professionals, and significantly increased the cost of education. It will be interesting to see if the current levels of legal involvement in education can be sustained as we enter a more restrictive financial environment for public schools.

8

Curriculum and Instruction—
The What and How of Schooling

The issues of "what is taught" and "how it is taught" are obviously important components affecting the quality of public education. There has been an unfortunate narrowing of the curriculum in recent decades because of an overemphasis on standardized testing of basic skills. Educators often have to fight against the testing mania championed by politicians and media pundits to maintain a healthy balance among different curricular subjects.

In the United States, curriculum standards are set at the state level so that we theoretically have fifty different sets of standards. Critics of American public education often lament the degree of variance that this implies and compare our system unfavorably with those of other industrialized nations. Actually, there is a fair degree of commonality among the fifty states in terms of state-mandated curriculum standards.

A consortium of forty-eight states is currently collaborating on the Common Core State Standards Initiative. On June 2, 2010, this group released a detailed list of knowledge students should acquire in language arts and mathematics. This effort should lead the United States closer to a unified curriculum on a national basis. While such a development is welcome, the larger problem is the extent to which any state or national curriculum is actually implemented at the local level.

The existing level of common curricula among the states is driven by three discrete factors. The first influence is the national organizations, either public or private, that develop curriculum standards for individual disciplines such as science, mathematics, and English. These guidelines often find their way into state requirements with little revision to the original recommendations. These professional organizations are much more active in recommending curriculum standards than they were fifty years ago. For a brief period in the 1990s the Department of Education attempted to develop national curriculum standards. This movement fell victim to political controversies over the history standards, eventually bringing the initiative to a halt.

Second, American schools are more dependent than schools in most countries on the textbook industry. This industry must meet the requirements of state-level textbook committees in several states that often determine what is required and what should be excluded from elementary and secondary school textbooks. State-level textbook committees in California and Texas are particularly influential since these boards must approve all textbooks used in these states. A large proportion of textbook sales occur in these two states with large student populations.

Textbook companies strive mightily to meet the requirements of the textbook committees in Texas and California. The textbooks, as adopted in these two states, are then made available to school districts across the country. Thus, to the extent that teachers use textbooks as the basis for instruction, there is a good deal of uniformity regarding what is taught in classrooms throughout the nation.

A further aspect on the impact of state textbook selection committees concerns the public stage these committee meetings afford special interest groups to attempt to impose their narrow agendas on the nation's schoolchildren. Groups as varied as gay rights advocates, environmentalist groups, and fundamentalist religious groups all pressure these state committees to include content that promotes their special interests. This type of controversy among members of the Texas Textbook Selection Committee achieved national notoriety in early 2010.

The state textbook committees often succumb to these pressures, thereby promoting propaganda where there ought to be unbiased educational information. Textbook publishers naturally seek to avoid offending any conceivable group. Ultimately they produce textbooks so bland and uninteresting that students find them virtually unreadable.

A third factor promoting commonality of curriculum among states is the associations of state-level school officials such as the National Association of State School Superintendents. These groups meet annually to share information on various curriculum development projects. These associations tend to foster a fairly uniform model of curriculum development across the nation. Given the nature of our federal system, we do have a relatively uniform curriculum across the country, with states reserving the final authority over curriculum content for their own schools.

One salutary influence on school curriculum over the past few decades has been the increase in the number of high school students taking advanced placement courses. These are college-level courses prepared by scholars in the seventeen fields in which they are offered. The final exams are prepared by the College Testing Service, given under very controlled conditions, and graded by objective evaluators outside the high school setting.

An unfortunate truth about curriculum in the United States is that many, if not most, school districts do not have an up-to-date curriculum that is implemented at the classroom level. Curriculum development is a longer-term issue that is often pushed aside by more urgent administrative concerns. While most teachers agree theoretically that a strong unified curriculum is desirable, many also exhibit the normal human proclivity to resist constraints on their work from above.

The most important issue is the extent to which good curricula are taught effectively. The curriculum at the elementary level is rather simple conceptually and there is little problem with teachers being able to teach the curriculum effectively. The exceptions to this generally sanguine view are in the areas of science and mathematics. Few elementary teachers are sufficiently knowledgeable in these two disciplines. Also, many elementary school principals are limited in the supervisory guidance that they can offer to teachers in these subject areas.

At the secondary school level the building administrators have come from the ranks of secondary teachers, and therefore they usually have a narrow curriculum competence only in their area of certification, be it language arts, science, math, or social studies. Some administrators come from backgrounds in physical education, the practical arts, and so on, and thus have little specialized knowledge in academic areas. Therefore, most secondary administrators are ill equipped to assist their teachers who may have weaknesses in core academic areas.

In fact, American public education has consistently suffered a shortage on minimally qualified instructors in science and math. About 20 percent of all math and science instructors nationally are not even minimally certified in their assigned teaching areas. This shortage is being exacerbated by the fact that certification requirements in many states are becoming more restrictive.

A principal reason for this chronic problem is what is known as the single-salary schedule. All teachers in a school district are paid the same according to years of experience and advanced degrees, regardless of supply-and-demand imbalances for given subject areas. It is comparatively easy to hire elementary, physical education, and social studies teachers at the beginning salary rate. They do not have as many options for higher pay in other industries.

Potential science and math teachers, on the other hand, often have job prospects outside education that can pay $10,000 to $20,000 more than the salary of a beginning teacher. Salary schedules are part of the formal teachers' contract that, in most states, must be voted upon and accepted by the majority of teachers in the school district. Since there are more teachers in subjects with an oversupply than subjects with an undersupply, the majority of teachers are unlikely to ratify a salary schedule with differential salaries according to supply and demand.

The No Child Left Behind Act does require that all teachers be "highly qualified," which is defined as having a more thorough knowledge of their teaching field than was required previously. This requirement has raised the qualifications of teachers to some extent, but has not materially increased the supply of new teachers.

Attracting teachers who are academically prepared to teach is a necessary but not sufficient condition to improve public education. Excellent teaching involves far more than simply knowing your subject well. The teacher needs to know how to convert difficult concepts into lessons that are understandable to the students at their current level of knowledge.

Good teachers also make a great effort to present the information in a manner that will engage the interest of the students. Most importantly, great teachers have a true interest in their students. This is critical at the elementary school level and still quite important at the high school level, although high school students are better able to differentiate between the teacher and the course.

Teachers can be trained to prepare better classes, instruct students at their current level of knowledge, create evaluation instruments that are fair and valid, and expend the time and energy necessary to be highly effective. Most importantly, however, teachers must have the character and personality traits that enable them to relate to students and serve as worthy adult role models. It is an interesting expectation, or perhaps hope, that at any given time there are more than three million Americans willing and able to provide every public school classroom with an excellent teacher.

To assert that teachers can be trained to be more effective begs the question as to the source of this training. The typical school administrator, particularly at the secondary level, actually spends very little time directly observing instruction and helping teachers to improve their practice. A middle school of eight hundred students, for example, will typically have a principal and one assistant principal.

The assistant principal will spend almost all of his or her time dealing with major and minor student discipline issues. This function is especially time-consuming in our modern era when a quasilegal approach needs to be taken with even minor disciplinary infractions. Assistant principals typically spend no more than 10 percent of their available energies directly supervising and coaching teachers on their teaching techniques.

A teacher may be observed during one or two class periods per year, with a conference held with the teacher before or after the classroom observation.

There are thousands of schools around the country where even these minimal supervisory benchmarks are honored in the breach. This minimalist supervisory protocol exists, in spite of the fact that most states require classroom observations and subsequent evaluation of teachers on a yearly basis.

The extent of teacher supervision at the high school level is similar to that in the middle schools. A high school of twelve hundred may have a principal and two assistant principals. The assistants will spend the major share of their time and energy on student disciplinary matters. Discipline problems become more serious at the high school level given drug abuse issues, threats against teachers, altercations among students, property theft and damage, and so on. Unfortunately, these serious disciplinary concerns are becoming more pronounced at both the middle school and elementary school levels.

Dealing with the more serious student issues in high schools often requires involvement by school district lawyers, court appearances, and suspension and expulsion hearings. Considering the myriad tasks that the modern school administrator must perform, it is somewhat surprising that the quality and extent of teacher supervision is actually moderately better than it was forty years ago.

A more general point about the school curriculum is that there are really three dimensions to curriculum implementation. There is the written curriculum, the taught curriculum, and the tested curriculum. Some districts that perform poorly on state tests simply fail to do an effective job of ensuring that the tested curriculum is also the taught curriculum.

Second, even when a district has a well-developed written curriculum, individual teachers often do not follow it faithfully. There are school districts where good curriculum materials exist, but are generally ignored by the classroom teacher. The degree to which teachers follow a prescribed curriculum, however, is somewhat better nationally than it was forty years ago.

Why is it that many school administrators do not insist that teachers follow the prescribed curriculum? The obvious answer is that many school administrators do a very superficial job of monitoring instruction. The teaching of the prescribed curriculum cannot be monitored effectively if only one or two classes per year are observed.

Elementary school principals tend to more closely monitor the classroom performance of their teachers and often require teachers to submit their lesson plans on a weekly basis. Such attention to lesson plans cannot be expected of principals in secondary schools because of the magnitude of their other tasks. Thus, under current staffing levels, it is very difficult for a school district to monitor the proper delivery of the written curriculum.

Unfortunately, there are still thousands of school districts in the United States where there are no written curriculum guidelines at the district level.

In these cases a teacher is left with the more general curriculum standards issued by the state and the implicit curriculum that is contained in the textbooks used by the teacher. Worse yet, in those districts lacking strong curriculum standards, too many teachers simply follow their own desires in terms of what is taught.

In discussing curriculum issues we need to address the so-called informal curriculum. This is what we teach students indirectly about how to be a decent human being and a good citizen. Teachers usually do this by the values that they espouse and live on a daily basis. There are literally hundreds of opportunities during a student's schooling where he can learn how to act like a responsible and caring adult through the behavior he sees exhibited by his teachers. Most teachers take their responsibilities as a role model very seriously.

Few teachers want to look back on their careers and conclude that their major accomplishment was to teach thousands of students the intricacies of subject-verb agreement or how to solve equations using the Pythagorean theorem. It is scandalous that public discussions about the importance of education are generally reduced to the issue of attaining basic academic skills. This is obviously important and essential, but it is not sufficient.

Good teachers inspire students to perform difficult academic work and to enjoy the learning process. Such teachers also derive great satisfaction from helping to develop the character and values of their students. Most teachers would say that these interactions are the most critical factors to their level of job satisfaction.

There is a disconnect between the focus of pundits and public officials regarding the centrality of student test scores in evaluating school success, and the more global view of teachers who see academic performance as a necessary but not sufficient benchmark for evaluating school success. It would require a sea change in teachers' and principals' attitudes for a majority of educators to accept the notion that their job is simply to improve student performance on standardized tests. Good education entails far more than is debated in the typical public discourse on the state of public education.

This review of curriculum and instruction reveals that school curriculum in the United States is determined by states and local districts rather than the national government. This allows for a greater diversity in curriculum than is found in other developed nations. This reality reinforces the American concept of local control but places our students at somewhat of a disadvantage when competing with other nations on standardized tests that assume a common curriculum. This variable quality of the written curriculum greatly affects the overall quality of education.

Teacher supervision in the United States is performed inadequately in most places and not at all in others. This lack of rigorous teacher supervision is primarily the result of insufficient administrative staff to perform the task well, as well as a tradition of considering the teacher to be the sole master of his or her classroom. American supervisory practices, however, do not vary greatly from the norm internationally (Organization for Economic Cooperation and Development, 2009, *Highlights*, 82).

This discussion highlights the disparity that exists between what practicing teachers and principals consider the important elements of a good education and what tends to be emphasized in the public discourse about education. Educators generally have a far more holistic view of education than do media pundits and commentators on the cultural and social scene. They seek to develop humane traits in students through literature and the arts. They attempt to inform the understanding of students through studies in history, geography, science, foreign languages, and economics. True educators want to prepare students for citizenship through studies in government, its potential, and its limits.

A good curriculum is both broad and deep. The development of a comprehensive curriculum on a national scale is one recommendation for improvement discussed in chapter 19, "Final Exam."

9

Students Then and Now

In the next several chapters we examine how school staff and school officials interact with their various constituencies. This provides a context for how the work of the public schools is conducted. No context is more important than the culture, attitudes, and assumptions that students bring to their educational experiences.

To begin with, students in all eras approach their schooling in a historical vacuum. To the average high school student of today, for example, September 11, 2001, barely registers on his or her consciousness. In the minds of many high school students, the invention of the iPod and the automobile are practically simultaneous events.

The thrust of this chapter is definitely not that today's young people are somehow inferior to students of previous generations. Criticism of the younger generation has been a propensity of elderly curmudgeons since the time of Socrates. The children of today are no better and no worse than any of the three generations of students attending school during the forty-five-year time frame under discussion.

Children today, however, are growing up in a world that is fundamentally different from the world of the 1950s, 1960s, or even the 1970s. One only has to witness a four-year-old child's facility with a TV remote to realize that today's young people have mastered skills that some adults still struggle with.

There is no doubt that the lifestyle of today's students has an impact on their interest and motivation to pursue academic content. Students arrive at kindergarten having watched five thousand to ten thousand hours of the high-energy, high-intensity fare of children's TV ranging from *Sesame Street* to the Cartoon Network. Mere toddlers can manipulate cartoon programs on a computer or video game. Many middle-class children grow up in a world of instant gratification where their meals come out of microwaves and where overindulgent parents tend to ensure that the child's every whim is gratified.

When this child enters the world of a school classroom, he or she finds the pace much slower and the intensity level much less than is experienced at home. The child must learn to subordinate his or her own impulses to the routines of a class of twenty-five students and one teacher. Most children can adapt to this radical change, but a significant number cannot. The pressure on children to adapt to a structured academic emphasis has found its way to kindergarten classrooms. Teachers of the early primary grades spend much of their time and energy on simply domesticating the troubling number of students who have difficulty adjusting to the demands of a businesslike classroom setting.

It is interesting that efforts to improve student achievement over the past several decades have been somewhat more successful at the elementary level than at the middle and high school levels. This discrepancy can be seen in the data on student achievement provided in chapter 3. One could make the argument that the more modest improvements at the middle and high school levels are a result of the older students being more influenced by the general culture than are the younger students.

By their early teens, students are less responsive to parental influence and more influenced by their peer group. The media culture intensifies the young person's identification with peer group versus parents. Elementary school students are more likely to respond positively to the urging of parents and teachers toward high academic achievement than are high school students.

How does the general culture impinge on children's consciousness as they approach adolescence? Almost twenty years ago, foreign Fulbright Exchange teachers who were working in the United States for one year were interviewed on their impressions of American students. Most of them expressed amazement at the number of distractions from school matters that American students experience. These vary from holding a part-time job to early romantic involvement to succumbing to drug and alcohol abuse. These foreign teachers reported that the impact of these factors on children in their home countries were less intense and intrusive than in the United States (McAdams, 1993).

Returning to the present we find that students are still subject to the old distractions but are now exposed to a host of new technologies that draw them away from their studies. Many middle-class students spend much time each day on a cell phone, Facebook, Twitter, and texting. A story in the *New York Times* of May 25, 2009, reported that the average teenager sent or received eighty text messages per day, double the number from only a year before (Hafner, 2009). The old saying about people wasting time by "frittering their life away" might need to be updated to observe that young people may be "twittering their life away."

A recent episode in a Canadian high school illustrates the growing problem of technological obsession. A boy was texting during class, despite repeated requests from his teacher to stop. The teacher eventually sent him to the principal's office to be disciplined. While the principal was reprimanding the student, the principal noticed that the student's arm and hand were moving under the principal's desk. Predictably, the student was texting his friends about being disciplined in the principal's office.

This is a serious issue. To become well educated requires self-discipline, concentration, and intense and constant effort. We know as adults the power of the Internet, e-mail, cell phones, and texting to divert our attention from our formal tasks. Checking for messages has become an obsession for many adults. How much more compulsive can using these technologies become for adolescents who are almost obsessively concerned with the attitudes and activities of their peers? We don't know the extent to which these new technologies have complicated the efforts of teachers, but there can be little doubt that the influence is not helpful to academic performance.

By the time they reach middle school, young people have spent thousands of hours watching videos and TV shows that portray parents and teachers in a less than flattering light. Fathers especially are portrayed as buffoons or worse in what passes for family comedies in today's media culture. Adults are not portrayed as being worthy of respect and emulation, so that today's young people naturally show no great desire to assume adult responsibilities.

We now speak of young people not being expected to assume full adult responsibilities until they are about thirty. From the perspective of a fifteen-year-old, full adulthood is literally a lifetime away. Adolescents are likely to conclude that they have plenty of time to get serious about both personal and career decisions.

Middle-class children in today's America are not driven by a need to lift themselves from grinding poverty, as might have been the case for the generation raised after the Depression. They have not experienced economic deprivation in any area of their life and fully expect to be economically successful, although they are hazy about just how this might happen. It is very instructive to see the difference in the attitude toward education of many first-generation immigrants who have escaped abject poverty in their home country, as compared with the attitude toward schooling of many middle-class American children.

The distractions and roadblocks to student achievement outlined previously are even more daunting for the 25 percent of students who live in disadvantaged communities, reside in troubled homes, and, not surprisingly, are often forced to attend failing schools. These students daily confront violence in their communities, alcohol and drug abuse in their families, and a peer culture that is openly hostile to school achievement.

The heroes in such communities tend to be rappers, professional athletes, and drug dealers. It takes acts of heroic courage for young people in such an environment to succeed in school. Students who do rise above these conditions illustrate the best that the human spirit can achieve.

We should not fault our young people who have such attitudes—these attitudes are to be expected given the world as our children experience it. The point is simply that motivating such children to high academic performance is more difficult than it is to motivate children who have a real thirst for education. The low bar that is set for admission to many colleges further reinforces a lackadaisical attitude toward academic performance by many students.

A Philly.com article of June 24, 2007, relates the story of one man's attempt to positively affect the future of children in an inner-city Philadelphia school (Mezzacappa, 2007). A wealthy and generous Connecticut businessman named George Weiss attempted to take an entire sixth-grade elementary school class in a Philadelphia ghetto and lift them beyond their circumstances through education.

In 1987 Weiss offered every one of the 112 graduates of Belmont Elementary School a free college education if they were able to graduate from high school. Over the following years Weiss donated $5 million to enable these students and their schools to provide supports such as extra tutoring and extra counseling services.

About 60 percent of these students ultimately graduated from high school and twenty of the students graduated from a four-year college. This is more than twice the number that would have achieved these goals absent Weiss's generosity. Weiss has continued similar programs in several other inner-city schools that have met with even higher success.

On the negative side of the ledger, it must be acknowledged that high school graduation rates and college attendance rates for students from Weiss's schools are still far below that of students from better socioeconomic backgrounds. Of the original sixth-grade class at Belmont, eight students are dead. By the time that the students reached high school, at least seventeen of the boys were dealing drugs. An unacceptable number of the students have been ensnared in the criminal justice system, including jail time for several of them. The sad truth here is that even with extraordinary attempts to save these students, too many of them fall victim to their larger dysfunctional community.

The John McDonough High School in New Orleans has reinvented itself in the aftermath of Hurricane Katrina. This is a success story in the midst of a totally collapsed community. The good news here is that schools can rise from the depths of disaster. The larger problem is that hundreds of communities in the United States are the victims of a social and economic slow-moving Katrina.

Almost every middle-class student now expects to go to college. The student expects his or her parents and the government to pay for college and expects to find a school amenable to whatever level of effort he or she is willing to expend. Most other highly developed nations have clear standards for high school graduation and college admission that are external to the schools themselves. Students in these countries must meet these rigorous standards if they wish to attend a college or university. In the United States we seem to believe that we should provide a seat at college for anybody who wishes to attend. Some politicians even assert that every student should attend college. This dynamic may explain why we have a large percentage of students who do not graduate from college, and those who do graduate require an average of six years to complete what is ostensibly a four-year program.

About 10–20 percent of our students do perform extremely well academically. These are the students who will attend highly selective colleges and universities and who aspire to careers in the most challenging professions. Such schools, however, are only a small percentage of all colleges available to students.

Watching about one hundred of the top academic students in a very upper-middle-class county competing with one another on quick recall of information and knowledge is very instructive. Students participating in these academic competitions were incredibly well informed on some very esoteric subjects, as well as the more common subjects that would have been a formal part of their education. It is absolutely inspiring to see these outstanding high school students from our local public schools.

These students are highly intelligent as well as self-motivated to excel in academics. Many of them came from homes with supportive parents, although some came from homes with parents who were not well educated themselves or who had no particular interest in education. The public schools do not deserve the primary credit for the extraordinary success of these students. The schools do, however, play a critical role in nurturing and supporting these students by providing the content and instructional strategies to optimize the achievement of these students.

Conversely, this dynamic impacts student who are much less motivated to succeed academically. The schools provide the content and appropriate instructional strategies and they attempt to nurture and support student learning. In many cases, however, neither the student nor his or her parents are interested in making the effort necessary for academic success. In most of

America's communities, highly successful as well as failing students attend the same high school. They often sit in the same classrooms with the same teachers. We must remember that students are free moral agents who will play the primary role in their own education.

High school principals frequently have parent conferences with the parents of students with serious academic or disciplinary problems. They meet a number of seemingly excellent parents who, nonetheless, were raising children with serious problems. On the other hand, they also meet some parents of outstanding students at awards ceremonies or National Honor Society inductions who don't seem to be particularly interested or involved with their child's education. There are more than a few cases where the parents of these successful students are not present to honor their child's academic success.

As a general rule, supportive and involved parents increase the odds that their children will perform well academically. The general rule, however, does not hold in all situations. The word *education*, after all, is related to the Latin word *educere*, which means to "bring out." This definition implies that education is something that you draw out of students, not something that you pour into them. We sometimes overlook the obvious truth that learning requires the cooperation of the student.

Studying successful charter schools in our inner cities illustrates the concept that successful schools draw out the student to participate actively in his or her own education. Students attending these schools are usually selected by lottery from among those students who apply for admission. They and their parents then sign a contract with the school promising to cooperate fully with school regulations and academic expectations.

Such pledges may include a commitment to regular attendance, completion of daily homework assignments often two hours in length, agreeing to wear the school uniform, and abiding by the high behavioral standard expected of students. In some charter schools engaging in fighting or other violent behavior can lead to expulsion. Because of legal constraints, such requirements are largely absent in regular public schools.

Examining the daily ethos in these charter schools calls to mind the way all schools operated in the 1960s and before. In those days disruptive students could ultimately be expelled—a very potent power exercised almost solely by the school principal. Also, while students did not wear uniforms, there were fairly strict dress codes. Through the late 1960s girls were still sent home to change if their skirts were too short. The dress code for girls in public schools required that they wear either a skirt or a dress—no jeans, slacks, or shorts. The purpose of these dress codes for both sexes, a code similar to what we consider "business casual" in today's world, was to instill a businesslike atmosphere in the schools that would positively influence student deportment.

Parents of disruptive students were required to meet with the principal before their suspended student could be readmitted to school. This procedure is still generally followed in public schools, although there is little that a school administrator can do if the parent refuses to meet with the principal. In some school districts a student is readmitted as soon as the parent arrives for the conference, even if it is only the first day of an assigned five-day suspension. More restrictive rules apply if an administrator seeks to suspend a special education student.

This compromising and undermining of the school's authority over the decades is mainly the result of state and federal court cases in the 1970s and 1980s. Judges readmitted students who had been expelled for behaviors in school that the same judge would never allow in his own courtroom. Building principals during the 1970s argued vociferously that these court-mandated changes would be detrimental to an orderly school environment, and ultimately harmful to the children. Any administrator from the 1970s working with today's generation of teachers and administrators would be struck by how hard their task is in today's schools compared with their predecessors forty-five years ago. Education is a much more challenging profession than it once was.

While reading about the school rules and expectations common to many inner-city charter schools, a school administrator from the 1970s may well experience an epiphany! In many ways the charter schools of today are re-inventing the public schools of the 1960s and before, the difference being that forty-five years ago disruptive students were removed from the public schools. In today's world, serious students are leaving the public schools for charter schools, leaving the disruptive and indifferent students behind.

Most public schools can assimilate the current legal constraints because most schools have relatively few seriously disruptive students. The education of other students is not materially affected. Once the number of disruptive students reaches a critical mass, however, as in many dysfunctional schools, the troubled students overwhelm the system and cause the school to fail all of its students.

In spite of all of the cultural distractions faced by our students, and despite the difficult legal constraints endured by teachers and administrators, most students in most places can and do receive a good-quality public education. We have reason to remain optimistic about the majority of our young people and their schools as we look to the future.

10

The Parent Factor

Recent decades have seen a noticeable shift in parental attitudes toward their children's education and schools. The majority of parents continue to maintain a healthy interest in the education of their children. Most parents continue to encourage their children and support their educational efforts to an appropriate degree. There are growing numbers of parents, however, at both ends of the parental engagement spectrum that are either totally detached from or overly involved with their children's education.

As noted in chapter 3, a greater proportion of public school students than previously arrive at school suffering from serious social, financial, or mental challenges. While many parents in these homes do struggle to see their children succeed in schools, it is undeniable that many of these parents themselves lead disorganized and distracted lives and have little energy or interest in the education of their children. This group represents about 20 percent of parents on a nationwide basis. When these disengaged parents and their children are concentrated in the same communities, we have a prescription for educational disaster.

Perhaps another 15 percent of parents send their children to decent schools in stable communities, but do not themselves place a high value on education. In some cases parents actually don't want their children to succeed academically for fear that the children will leave home for college and never return to live in their home community. These parents see their children's school success as a threat to their way of life. Some parents value their home community and a close family above career or economic success for themselves or their children.

Students from these families do graduate from high school but are not motivated or encouraged to excel academically. These same high schools produce other students who are academic high achievers who then proceed to follow a life of high career achievement. The great majority of high schools in small towns and small cities around the country seek to successfully educate a student body destined to experience widely diverse life trajectories.

These are the communities where parents are more likely to complain that academic standards are too strict rather than too lax. Most school principals and superintendents receive at least ten times as many complaints from parents about unreasonably high standards as they do about standards that are too lax. Some parents consistently complain that their child's teacher is too strict, too demanding, or is not an effective instructor. While such complaints are sometimes valid, in most cases the initial problem is a lack of effort on the part of the student.

Of course, the majority of parents remain extremely supportive of schools and teachers. In recent years, however, we have witnessed a new phenomenon in a subset of this supportive group known as "helicopter parents." These parents hover over their children to such an extent that their children don't have the opportunity to solve their own normal school-related problems. Instead, such parents interject themselves into the operation of the schools and the life of their children to an unhealthy degree. Such parents are somewhat problematic to school staff members, but they definitely interfere with the progress of the student toward responsible adulthood.

A superintendent encountered just such a helicopter parent in a recent meeting. She was a parent of a seventh-grade boy who had been cut from the middle school basketball team. She complained to the coach and then to the building principal. Finally, she asked to see the superintendent. She began the meeting by presenting a copy of her child's résumé—this for a thirteen-year-old seventh-grade student.

This résumé listed all of the various athletic achievements of the boy, none involving basketball. She argued that this proved that the coach was somehow biased against her son. She had no supporting evidence for this charge. Needless to say, the superintendent was unable to accommodate the mother's demand that the child be placed on the basketball team.

Sometimes parents are right when they accuse teachers of being too demanding or unfair to their students. School officials should always give parents the benefit of the doubt, investigate the allegations, and take corrective action when necessary. It is also true that many school administrators are too protective of their teachers in such situations. There are countless cases, however, when the students are in the wrong and the teachers are simply trying to apply a reasonable level of rigor to their courses.

Such conscientious teachers are trying to meet their obligations to provide a high-quality education to their students. Unfortunately, some students and parents, while concerned about achieving good grades, wish to do so with minimal effort. In our educational system, access to a good college is highly dependent on the grades that students earn while in high school. For this reason, some parents view teachers with high standards as a roadblock for their children and students view the teacher more like an umpire than like a coach.

In the book *Lessons From Abroad* comparing six school systems, including that of the United States, it is noted that many highly developed countries require that students take national achievement tests before finishing secondary school. Students must earn a certain grade on these tests before being eligible for admission to a college or university. In these countries the teacher is seen more as a coach than an umpire. Teachers and students are more likely to work collaboratively to provide students the necessary knowledge and skills to succeed on these national tests. This makes the entire dynamic among teachers, students, and parents more positive and cooperative than is often the case in the United States.

The consumerist and competitive approach characteristic of American culture applies to our educational practices. While other highly developed countries have limits to the number of universities that they allow and support, the United States keeps expanding colleges and increasing enrollment to meet the perceived demand. Only in America do you hear politicians asserting that every student should attend college.

In this demand-side scenario, we expand college enrollments even if it means that we must lower admission standards to accommodate the increasing numbers of young people now attending college. Furthermore, the overemphasis on college has contributed to the high school dropout rate by eliminating vocational training options that were common in previous eras.

Even well-respected universities now provide remedial reading and writing programs to bring lower-achieving students to an academic threshold where they can succeed with college-level work. Basic academic skills should be mastered before students arrive at college, and colleges should not admit students unless and until they have reached the standard of academic achievement necessary to pursue college-level instruction.

The lowered standards and expanded remedial opportunities still yield a disappointing record for colleges in terms of graduation rates. College is designed to be a four-year journey toward a bachelor's degree. The *USA Today* issue of June 3, 2009, reports that four-year colleges graduate only 53 percent of their students within six years (Marklein, 2009). This baleful headline number obscures the fact that many colleges graduate only 30 to 40 percent of their students within six years. About one-third of students who start college never earn a degree.

These practices generate a heavy burden in educational costs for the student, his family, and the state and federal government. Millions of college graduates and dropouts become chained to large debt levels. Their lack of readily marketable skills condemns many students to many years of lower living standards as they struggle to repay their loans.

Most American parents assume that it is the job of the school to remediate any academic deficiencies on the part of their students. Many American parents reject the notion, at least subconsciously, that it is primarily the task of the student to overcome challenges, rather than the responsibility of the schools to remediate academic deficiencies. Many immigrant parents, however, insist that their children assume the burden of performing very well in schools that are foreign to them.

An example of this phenomenon occurred more than thirty-five years ago in an affluent and academically rigorous suburban Philadelphia school district. A tenth-grade Asian immigrant arrived in September without being able to speak a word of English. By June he was among the top students in his class academically. This required an enormous effort on the part of the student, especially since the high school in question had a large number of high-performing students.

Today there are a myriad of academic supports in most public schools for students performing below their grade level, for whatever reason. On one hand it is commendable that schools can provide such supports. On the other hand, these extra instructional services come at a high price, increasing the overall cost of education. Much of the additional cost of education in recent decades can be traced to increasing expectations for the schools and decreasing expectations for students and their parents.

Whereas forty-five years ago about 20 percent of all students came from backgrounds and personal disadvantages that made academic success problematic, today the percentage of such students nationwide is notably higher. Affluent middle-class couples that, on average, would provide homes supportive of education are having fewer children than was the case forty-five years ago. Two-income couples with high academic aspirations for their children typically have only one or two children. Many well-educated couples are childless by choice.

A disproportionate percentage of students in private schools come from middle or upper middle-class homes. This further weakens the academic potential of schools with large numbers of disadvantaged children. A case can be made that, given the handicaps faced by teachers in today's public schools, it is a tribute to educators that academic achievement has improved at all over the years.

Let's explore specific ways in which some problematic parents can undermine serious academic standards in our public schools. Generally speaking, today's parents express an overriding concern that their children enjoy, or at least be contented, in their school experience. Simultaneously, parents want their children to be educated well enough to compete successfully in college admissions and the workforce. Knowledge, in the abstract, is not a priority for these parents. Given this mind-set, how is it that some parents unintentionally undermine rigorous academic standards in the schools?

Parents actively undermine the academic mission of the schools sometimes at junior or senior high school–level science fairs. It often becomes painfully obvious that some of the projects were the work of parents, some of them engineers, rather than the work of a fifteen-year-old student. One can imagine the message to students who did do their own projects. Of course, it is useless to accuse the parent of doing the project since he or she would claim total innocence or that only incidental assistance was provided.

Particularly at the elementary school level, parents sometimes pressure the principal to place their students in the class of a popular teacher, or at least avoid placing their child in the class of an unpopular teacher. Sometimes these parental preferences are well founded since there obviously are some teachers who are not as effective as could be desired. Often, however, parents seek to avoid certain teachers because they are too demanding on the students or because they do not have the warm personality that appeals to children and their parents. Often these more demanding teachers, personable or otherwise, are actually doing an excellent job in eliciting the best effort from students.

Parents also undermine rigorous standards by complaining that a given teacher has testing and evaluation standards that are too demanding. Their children are receiving lower grades than the parents expect. Too many parents immediately conclude that the teacher is unreasonable, rather than that their child is not putting forth a reasonable effort. Again, sometimes parents are correct in this assessment and therefore such complaints should be investigated by the building principal.

Often, however, the teacher is not being unreasonable but the students simply are not willing to exert the necessary effort. If enough students perform at a mediocre level the pressure is on the teacher, since too many poorly performing students are viewed as a reflection on the teacher rather than the students. In some instances principals will actually pressure their teachers to lower their expectations of students, even when such expectations are reasonable.

Parents are also wont to complain that their students have too much home-work or need to study too hard or too long to earn good test grades. This complaint is more often found at the secondary level. There are many high school courses, particularly in science and math, which require serious study to master successfully. In some cases students have been enrolled in courses where their background, ability, or level of effort are simply insufficient to ensure academic success. Here again parents too often conclude that the teacher is at fault rather than their student.

An additional source of parental complaint is a perception that the curriculum being taught is irrelevant or inappropriate for the age or academic level of the student. Again, sometimes parents are correct in this analysis. More frequently, however, the parent is really saying that since the curriculum apparently does not engage the child's interest, obviously the curriculum is the problem and not the lack of application on the part of the child.

In these scenarios, the parents are not intentionally trying to lower academic standards. They are merely reacting as parents instinctively do in the case of their individual child. It is only human for parents to assume that academic problems of their children are caused by factors external to the child or the home. Collectively, however, these parental pressures subtly undermine the academic mission of the schools.

America is a consumerist society with a deeply ingrained belief that the customer is always right. George Bernard Shaw once said, "Democracy is that form of government that ensures that people are never governed better than they deserve." The same can be said for schools. Our schools can never perform better than the parents of the students allow. It should not be surprising that communities with parents who make reasonable academic demands on their children enjoy schools where high student achievement is the norm.

Another pressure that parents bring to bear is an increasing tendency to threaten a lawsuit if they are displeased with their child's education. We are all familiar with the health care scenario where doctors practice defensive medicine in an effort to deflect lawsuits against them. This phenomenon raises the cost and complexity of health care. The same dynamic, albeit at a more modest level at this point, is beginning to affect school practices.

Teachers and principals are expending increasing amounts of time and energy to document their activities to demonstrate conclusively that they are meeting all legal obligations with respect to their students' educational program. This adds to the cost of education and adds an additional level of tension to the teacher's work life. In some communities, the pressures that parents place on teachers are so great that teachers are not permitted to meet with parents unless a guidance counselor or administrator is present.

There are several ways that educators may respond to a scenario where overly critical parents make life difficult for the teacher. Few of us, including teachers, are particularly courageous or assertive in our work life encounters. There is a tendency for many teachers to take the easier option of setting academic expectations for their students lower than they otherwise might be. Such teachers make few out-of-class assignments. Testing is either sporadic or is not sufficiently rigorous.

Standards of classroom discipline are more relaxed than is desirable. This diminishes the need for these teachers to send students to the principal's office or contact parents to discuss the student's unacceptable behavior. Teachers who operate in this manner seldom if ever generate complaints from either parents or students. The problem is that educational quality is compromised.

The principal sometimes supervises a teacher who is ineffective but never generates complaints from parents or students. This type of teacher typically shows a lot of videos and gives the students busywork to avoid preparing lessons or providing direct instruction. He or she also has very loose disciplinary standards. By simply passing the classroom in the hallway, an observer can see that little real learning is taking place. In many cases, a principal can quietly counsel the teacher out of the profession.

Unfortunately, there are thousands of similar situations across the nations that are chronically ignored. Such teachers simply remain below the radar, collect their paychecks, and ultimately retire with a good pension. A reasonable estimate is that at any given time about 10 percent of teachers fall into this category.

A second category of teachers successfully imposes ambitious academic standards because they are excellent teachers and can motivate students to perform at a high level. Even these teachers invite skepticism from some parents because the parents think that the teacher's expectations are higher than they should be. Such parents often keep their reservations to themselves because their children enjoy the classes and are obviously learning a good deal. Perhaps 25 percent of teachers fall into this category at any given time.

The last and largest category of teachers, encompassing two-thirds of all teachers, are those who try to impose reasonably high standards but are not gifted enough to inspire and motivate their students to the highest achievement level. These teachers incur some pushback from both students and parents and must continuously justify their demands to individual parents. This creates an ongoing tension in the work life of the teacher and militates against the teacher imposing standards quite as high as he or she would prefer.

This review begs the question as to why we do not have more excellent teachers. We need to consider the possibility that there simply are not enough potentially excellent teachers to staff every classroom in the nation.

The fact is that we must work with and support the teaching cadre that we have. The expectation that we can somehow recruit an extra five hundred thousand or more excellent teachers under current conditions represents the triumph of hope over experience.

What role do building-level administrators play with respect to parents? The number of parents exerting unreasonable pressures on her or his school sometimes overwhelms a school principal. It is not surprising that some principals, with limited intestinal fortitude, actually encourage their teachers to bend their standards so as to decrease parental complaints. Additionally, there is a strong tendency for a principal to circle the wagons when a teacher is attacked.

As in all professions, there is a natural instinct to react protectively when a member of the staff is attacked from without. Teachers highly value a principal who defends the teacher against unfair attacks from parents, students, or the general public. Not all principals are willing to correctly distinguish between teachers who should be supported and teachers who have valid parental complaints levied against them.

The previous examples of undue parental influences on the schools serve to undermine student achievement. Although the absolute number of problematic parents is not large, they can have an outsized negative effect on school and student achievement. American education would be improved if teachers and school officials had more authority and discretion to impose reasonable achievement standards on all students. Suggestions for stronger homework policies and a more rigorous curriculum are offered in chapter 19, "Final Exam."

11

The Limits of Local Control

When average citizens consider school governance, they think of their local school board and district and building administrators. There are more than fourteen thousand school districts in the United States ranging in size from several hundred students in rural communities to more than one million students in New York City. School boards of from three to fifteen members, usually elected by the citizens, typically govern these local school districts. In some jurisdictions such as larger cities, the mayor or city council appoint school boards. While it is true that these governing bodies manage the schools on a daily basis, major policy and strategic decisions are made at the state or federal level.

Under the U.S. Constitution, education is one of the powers reserved to the states under the Tenth Amendment. The first law governing education was the Old Deluder Satan Act of 1647 in Massachusetts. This law required that each community of fifty or more families pay a teacher to instruct children in basic reading and writing so that they could read the Bible. For the next two hundred years, education was conducted and directed primarily at the local level.

It was not until the second half of the nineteenth century that Horace Mann in Massachusetts and Chester Barnard in Connecticut championed statewide governance of the schools. These initiatives eventually led to complex state school codes throughout the United States designed to control most aspects of public education. It wasn't until the last decades of the nineteenth century that states began to mandate the establishment of high schools.

The limited communications and transportation technologies of the nineteenth century made it necessary for state educational laws to be administered locally as a matter of practicality. The position of superintendent of schools evolved from that of a state official to supervise and monitor schools at the county level to today's practice where a school superintendent, although in many states a state official, is appointed locally. Among his or her duties, the superintendent must ensure that state laws relating to curriculum, staffing, and finances are implemented faithfully at the local level. Few local citizens, including school board members, however, view their superintendent as in any sense a state official.

With the transportation and communications available to state departments of education over the past half-century, states can and do exercise far more direct control over the operation of local school districts than previously. A school superintendent today receives a steady stream of directives and reporting requirements from various bureaus within the state department of education. Local school officials spend 10–15 percent of their time responding to state directives, reporting requirements, or inquiries.

Examples of this growing state involvement include state requirements regarding student rights and responsibilities in the 1970s, and higher graduation and curriculum requirements following the *A Nation At Risk* federal report on the deficiencies of the public schools in the 1980s. States began mandating high-stakes testing requirements in the 1990s. These were followed by the requirements of the federal No Child Left Behind initiative in the first decade of this century. The No Child Left Behind Act, though a federal law, required each state to implement standardized testing and remediation efforts.

The spate of regulations in most states in the 1970s was mainly the result of Supreme Court and federal court decisions. Supreme Court decisions such as *Tinker vs. DesMoines* (1969) greatly expanded the rights of students vis-à-vis school officials. Elaborate guidelines were developed in the various states that required principals and other school officials to institute quasilegal procedures for investigating even relatively minor student infractions of school rules.

Most educators believe that much of the decline in the good discipline that formerly characterized public schools can be traced to these regulations that significantly handicapped teachers and school administrators in maintaining proper discipline. Clearly some abuses were prevented in this way, but the costs in time, effort, money, and to the learning environment are high.

The Nation At Risk federal report of 1983 was a damning indictment of the quality of American public schools versus those of other industrialized countries (National Commission on Excellence in Education, 1983). The report characterized the performance of our schools as a unilateral disarmament in world competitiveness. State politicians responded by raising graduation requirements and implementing more specific requirements for various curriculum areas to be implemented at the local level.

Shortly after these higher graduation requirements were enacted in one state, a highly placed state official questioned a superintendents' group about the impact on student achievement. He asked whether or not Scholastic Aptitude Test (SAT) scores had improved. This question was asked mere months after the new state requirements were passed and at least several years before they could conceivably have an effect on the SAT scores of high school seniors.

Furthermore, SAT scores are meant to predict the performance of students in their first year of college and are not achievement tests in the traditional meaning of the term. Thus we had a top state official showing no understanding of the likely impact of the new law. This anecdote is not meant as a harsh criticism of the official. It merely illustrates that the intricacies of school curricula and graduation requirements seldom engage the attention and understanding of state politicians, who are typically distracted by more urgent issues.

By the 1990s it was apparent that the higher graduation requirements and the curriculum initiatives of the 1980s were not having a significant effect on student performance. Most states began releasing student test scores by district in an attempt to bring public pressure to bear on local school districts to improve results. Not surprisingly, under-resourced school districts with a preponderance of disadvantaged students performed poorly on the tests, while schools in more affluent areas performed very well. This dynamic continued unabated throughout the 1990s.

Federal involvement in public education has expanded rapidly in recent decades. Before the creation of the Department of Education in the Carter administration, there was only a small federal bureau of education charged mainly with data collection functions. The first major educational law in recent times was the Title I law passed in 1965. This was part of President Johnson's Great Society program and was designed to provide preschool and supplemental instruction to students from disadvantaged backgrounds. Federal Head Start programs initiated in this period continue to serve families and children well.

This program expanded greatly over the decades, and by 2009 Title I enjoyed an annual federal budget allocation of $14 billion. Since the 1970s, other federal laws such as Title IX dealing with equal access to school programs for women, as well as the Education of All Handicapped Act relating to special education, have greatly expanded the role of federal laws in the daily operation of the schools.

Many of these federal laws and related state regulations trigger frequent state audits of school districts to ensure that the laws are followed faithfully. These audits increased paperwork dramatically at the local district level and require more administrative staffing to monitor and report on the programs. Because the programs are implemented at the building level, the time demands on both teachers and principals have also expanded greatly over the years.

Implementing these federal laws has complicated the daily operation of the schools since the various programs often deal with the same population of students and sometimes interfere with other aspects of the educational process. For example, it is not uncommon to have the same student eligible for multiple services such as English-as-a-second-language (ESL) instruction for language learners, Title I services for disadvantaged students underperforming in basic skills, or special education services for students with an identified special education disability.

A good example of this phenomenon is the necessity to conduct so-called "pullout programs" to provide services to Title I students, special education students, and ESL students. Consider a third-grade teacher with twenty-five students who must deal with the fact that two or three students are coming and going at any given time while she is trying to conduct a lesson in arithmetic. How does she replace the instruction that students miss because they have been pulled out of class for special services?

Keep in mind that the students most in need of basic instruction are the very ones removed from their regular class for special services. There is also a concern that younger children must interact with several additional adults in addition to their regular teacher. In many cases they might be better served by interacting with fewer adults at any given time.

These realities demonstrate that local school districts are increasingly controlled and monitored by both the state and federal government. Local school boards must formally accept many of the audits of school district operations mentioned previously. School boards must agree to take remedial action as directed by these audits or lose state or federal funding. In extreme cases, a school board may be liable for fines or legal action. Implementing these directives often has unanticipated impacts on other aspects of a school's operation, sometimes to the detriment of the student body as a whole.

Most of the changes in curriculum in recent decades have been driven by state and federal regulations and guidelines. Local school boards exercise little actual control over what is taught in district classrooms. Furthermore, the school board has virtually no control over instruction—the actual delivery of curriculum by teachers. As noted previously, even school principals have little time to devote to monitoring instruction in the classrooms. If principals can't adequately monitor what is happening in the classroom, how significant an impact can school board members or central office administrators have on the quality of instruction?

One area where the public assumes that local school boards have significant control is with the construction of school facilities. In virtually all states the state department of education participates at some level in funding school construction. The price for this state subsidy is a plethora of regulations and guidelines about what can be built, where it can be built, and how much can be spent. In Pennsylvania there are strict guidelines about the size of the campus for elementary and secondary schools, the physical dimensions of classrooms, and the square footage allowed for storage and other noninstructional areas.

Local school officials must repeatedly meet with state bureaucrats, along with the school district architect, to secure state approval for the proposed project. The school board must approve each stage of the submission of documents, even though the school board typically has little impact on the details of the project itself. This is not to argue that this level of state control is unwarranted. It merely illustrates the point that while it may appear from the outside that a school board can exercise substantial control over construction projects, the reality is quite different.

Even the school budget leaves relatively little room for decision making on the part of the school board. About 70 percent of the school budget is personnel-related. The school board is obligated to meet the requirements of its labor agreements and state laws in terms of salary increases and fringe benefits. It might be argued that the school board gets to negotiate what the salary and benefits increases will be, but that is only true in a formal sense.

In states with strong unions, one district is compared with other nearby districts and the final salary settlements are virtually identical with neighboring districts. Parents of school students indirectly or overtly pressure school boards to accede to teacher salary demands rather than have their students suffer from work slowdowns or stoppages.

Other school employee groups such as secretaries and custodians, while not wielding the same power as the teachers union, manage to be awarded salary increases that track closely those of teachers. School boards typically try to avoid the interorganizational jealousies and tensions that would occur if one category of workers were treated differently than other bargaining groups.

Because these negotiated contracts are for public employees at the local level, each group of employees has its own advocates in the community that exert pressure on school board members. Thousands of citizens have been elected to school boards on the promise that they will better control employee salaries. They almost always fail in this mission.

The remaining 30 percent of school district budgets relate to maintenance functions, utilities, transportation, and other relatively intractable expenses. In reality, a school board only has meaningful control over a small percentage of the budget—mainly textbooks, supplies, and other instructional materials. This is the first area where budget cuts are made because such reductions cause the least amount of public controversy. After two or three years, however, these cuts must be restored or the students and teachers will lack the basic tools of instruction. Sustained cuts in this portion of the budget is the equivalent of hiring a top-notch carpenter to build a house, but not giving him the hammer and nails he will need to do the job.

Over a ten-year period a local school district budget might increase by 50 percent. An especially fiscally conservative school board might have held the increase to 46 percent while a more liberal spending school board may have authorized an increase of 54 percent. Most school boards are a mix of fiscal conservatives and liberals so that the extremes cancel each other out over a ten-year period, thus producing the hypothetical 50 percent budget increase.

From time to time a school board produces budgets at one extreme or another along the fiscally liberal to conservative continuum. Such boards are usually voted out of office and replaced by board members that will bring expenses back toward the center.

As if these realities do not sufficiently constrain school board decision making, school boards in most states do not have the independent ability to set tax rates. In some states school board tentative budgets need to be approved by local municipal authorities or by county officials. In other states school budgets must be submitted to a public referendum. In any case the local school board has little real control over the level of spending.

We have seen that local school boards have relatively little control over school budgets, personnel decisions, curriculum, and instruction. How then do school boards spend their time and energy? If we analyze the topics that typically find their way to a school board agenda, we see that board meetings deal broadly with three types of issues.

The first of these activities include routine approvals of bill lists, personnel actions, and the approval of reports to be forwarded to state and federal agencies. A second category includes presentations from school administrators or teachers on school programs and recognitions of achievements for various students, teachers, and school-related groups. Individual board members serving as liaisons to countywide agencies such as technical schools or special education agencies also present reports to their board colleagues.

The final category of school board activity is what might be called "recurring conflicts." The start of the new school year typically finds parents complaining to the school board about some aspect of busing for their children. Later in the year a small cadre of citizens will attend budget meetings to complain about the high tax rates. Throughout the year individual groups will pressure the board to allocate more resources to their special interests.

These vary across a wide spectrum from a request for new uniforms for the high school band to more staffing resources for the gifted program.

In one otherwise excellent school district, the school board and community spent about twenty hours at public meetings over a period of several months engaging in heated arguments about whether the surface for a middle school athletic field should be artificial grass or real turf. This argument persisted in some form for well over one year. The intense emotions generated by such issues often lead to some turnover in board membership. It is on such issues that school board members are most often judged as they seek reelection.

School boards tend to exercise maximum control over issues that have only a tenuous connection to the educational program. These include topics such as bus routes, band uniforms, or athletic field surfaces. These issues do need to be decided with some reference to the opinions of the community. There is no other place that they could reasonably be resolved except at the local level. The most positive gloss that can be placed on these decisions is that they are important politically to the cohesion of the community, but they certainly have little to do with the educational program.

What impact then do school boards actually have? While school boards exert little direct control over education, they can and do influence the quality of school district performance. They do this primarily through the leadership tone and example that they set for the enterprise. Their first and most important task is to attract and employ an excellent superintendent. A good school board treats citizens, parents, teachers, and administrators with respect at all time.

The board respects the expertise of its professionals but does not blindly accept their judgments and proposals. Such a board asks its administrative staff to present its reports and recommendations in a complete and understandable manner and questions proposals that do not seem to be well supported.

Such school boards conduct their own internal business with integrity and competence. The board allows its administrators wide discretion, yet performs its oversight function as conscientiously as possible. A school board acting in this manner exudes a sense of competence and confidence that is communicated to staff and community. School employees have a sense of security knowing that their schools are being led in a sound matter, making the educational product better than it would otherwise be. Unfortunately, the benefits of a good school board are so diffuse that the average person cannot readily recognize the service that effective boards render to their community.

A poorly performing school board, on the other hand, can quickly demoralize a school district and will have a negative effect on the educational program. The unfortunate reality is that a good school board can be a catalyst to a gradually improving a school district over a period of five years or so, whereas a dysfunctional school board can negatively affect the educational program in less than a year.

At any given time about 25 percent of school boards are performing quite well while another 25 percent of school boards are very dysfunctional. The remaining school boards exhibit a middling level of performance. Over time most school boards in most districts swing from good to bad and back again. The problem is that it takes far longer for a school district to recover from a poor school board than it does for a well-functioning district to deteriorate under a dysfunctional board.

The takeaway concept from this discussion is that school boards cannot *control* schools in the technical sense of the term, but they do influence school district operations in ways that can materially affect school district quality. In this sense school boards are very important elements in school district operation. It is regrettable that political leaders, pundits, and educational researchers seldom consider the impact of the local school board on the quality of public education.

12

School Boards

More than one hundred thousand citizens serve on America's fourteen thousand school boards at any given time. Two-thirds of them serve without compensation. Board members who are compensated usually come from the larger urban districts, with their salary seldom exceeding $10,000. Board members serve for about seven years, on average. They are better educated than the general public and tend to represent their communities in ethnic and racial terms. About 60 percent of board members are men.

Board members average twenty-five hours per month in school district–related activities while a smaller number of board members spend up to twenty hours a week on board business. Most boards consist of from five to eight members with about 20 percent of boards having nine or more members. Citizens directly elect about 94 percent of board members (Hess, 2002, 3–5).

Hotly contested partisan politics can be found in urban school districts, but are far less common in the majority of smaller suburban and rural districts. School board elections tend to revolve around specific issues and are not necessarily driven by party affiliation. Most school board members tend to be conservative in their approach to school issues. The top concerns of board members early in the twenty-first century revolve around student achievement and school finances.

WELL-FUNCTIONING SCHOOL BOARDS

The great majority of school boards perform their duties in a fair to excellent manner. The fundamental truth relating to school governance echoes

Churchill's statement that "democracy is the worst form of government, except for all the rest." Ultimately a community will have the school board that it deserves. Local operation of the schools is deeply ingrained in our political traditions and almost certainly will continue into the future.

The single most important function of a school board is to recruit and retain a school superintendent to serve as the CEO of the district. The importance of this position for school district performance, district reputation, and staff morale cannot be overstated. This implies that a school board should focus on hiring a superintendent who will best meet the educational needs of the community. This person should be well versed in educational issues, be a responsible financial steward, and interact well with the school board, staff, and general community. In terms of character, the person should be of the highest integrity and should have the courage of his or her convictions.

A good school board should also pay close attention to its other central office administrators and particularly to its building administrators. Most board members interact regularly with central office administrators at school board meetings and more directly at board committee meetings such as personnel, curriculum, finance, and school facilities.

Effective boards soon come to recognize the special knowledge that business administrators, personnel directors, facility managers, and curriculum specialists can bring to the table on issues involving school board decision making. Less obvious to school board members is the importance of building-level administrators such as principals and assistant principals.

The school principal is really the only member of a building-level staff that the school board can reasonably expect will be focused on district-level initiatives and policies. Furthermore, this interest will only be stimulated in a district where the superintendent places district-level interests among the goals of the principal. Left to their own devices, school principals are understandably concerned with the effective operation of their own school rather than the broader concerns of the district. Only the superintendent and the school board are in a position to nurture district-wide thinking in their building principals.

An effective school board realizes that implementation of district policies and initiatives require the cooperation and energy of the building principal. A classroom teacher is primarily concerned with the instructional program for her or his students and with the smooth operation and good discipline of her or his local school. The teacher's next concern is with the welfare of fellow teachers and with the teacher's relationship with the building administrators.

Teachers seldom concern themselves with the priorities of the superintendent and rarely think about the goals of the school board and the district as a whole. This is not a criticism but merely reflects the reality that frontline personnel in any organization are primarily focused on their day-to-day activities and concerns.

How then can a school board infuse the priorities and goals of the district at the building level? The answer is through the efforts of the principal. An effective school board can engage building principals through periodic joint team-building and training programs. These often occur in the evening with a dinner followed by a one- to two-hour structured session on a selected topic. These occasions provide principals and board members with a less formal setting to discuss school matters. This minimal investment of time and effort by school board members may bear fruit with more extensive interactions between superintendents and principals designed to highlight district goals throughout the school year.

Effective board members should also visit the schools from time to time for athletic events, back-to-school nights, musical presentations, and other public occasions. Board members may also visit the schools during regular sessions, assuming their visits are conducted discreetly and in no way create discomfort among school staff members. Over time, effective board members should strive to develop a close enough rapport with building administrators so that administrators will feel free to discuss issues of substance with the board member.

The focus of board-member involvement with principals and schools should be the success of the educational program. This, of course, is the area where board members tend to have little experience, whereas educators feel that they have both the experience and the expertise. Board members must follow a very delicate path so that they are viewed as supportive and interested in quality education without at the same time interfering with the delivery of the educational program.

A school board member should concentrate on the ends of the instructional program rather than on the means to deliver it. The best way for school boards to exercise this oversight function of the instructional program is through participation in board-level curriculum committees. A second avenue for board members to emphasize student performance is to encourage reports by staff members at school board meetings featuring both hard and soft data on student achievement. A third way to influence instruction is for the board to establish benchmarks for student achievement and growth in various curriculum areas.

There is a very interesting phenomenon concerning student performance that affects school boards as well as the community that they serve. For decades now, the annual Gallup survey of citizen attitudes toward schools has shown a dichotomy between people's opinion of their own schools versus their opinion of public education in general. Citizens consistently rate their own schools and districts more positively than they rate public schools overall (some troubled urban districts excepted). This phenomenon can be attributed to what Garrison Keillor dubbed the "Lake Wobegon Effect." He lyrically speaks of the mythical Lake Wobegon of his Prairie Home Companion radio program where "all of the children are above average."

Parents and other citizens have a vested interest in their schools having a reputation for high quality. The perception of good community schools reinforces the decision of parents to move into a particular community and also raises property values for all homeowners in the school district. There is more than a little hometown boosterism in people's attitudes toward their schools. School board members share this attitude with even more intensity because they are charged with overseeing the quality of the local schools.

This view of the community schools through rose-colored glasses accounts for the virtual indifference among citizens, parents, and school board members to the constant procession of critical reports on the state of public education. Americans have been fed a steady diet of books and reports attempting to demonstrate that the performance of our public schools is mediocre at best. After fifty years, we need to accept the fact that, right or wrong, the general public is not dissatisfied with the performance of its public schools. School boards simply reflect this complacent attitude among most members of the general public.

Another characteristic of effective school boards is that they serve as ambassadors of the schools to the community. Through conversations with neighbors at barbeques and cocktail parties, board members increase the level of accurate information about the schools within the community. These infusions of reality blunt many of the more unflattering stories about the schools that are a topic of gossip in any community.

School board members can help citizens form more informed opinions about issues currently facing the schools. This can be particularly helpful in situations where an individual teacher or administrator is being unfairly attacked by a parent who feels ill served by a school employee. It is disconcerting to observe the level of bad feeling toward the schools that can be generated by a handful of unreasonable critics.

As noted in the previous chapter, school boards actually have little control over school finances. Effective board members realize this, and avoid making budget cuts that seem attractive in the short term but that can be very harmful over the long term. Cutting the budget for textbook and supplies is one example of short-term thinking. The most common example of this, however, is the significant financial impact of deferring necessary maintenance of facilities.

Delaying needed roof repairs year after year, for example, guarantees that before too long the general budget will be overwhelmed with expensive repairs, leaving insufficient funds available for the core mission of the schools. School budgets can only be nudged slightly upward or downward in any given year. Therefore, it behooves school board members to carefully consider how they want to invest the small degree of discretionary funds actually available in any single budget cycle.

A good school board should have at least a few financially astute members to monitor school district finances closely. Problems sometimes occur due to administrative malfeasance, but more often financial problems occur because of inertia and inattention. These board members should have access to detailed financial reports on a monthly basis and should carefully review annual audit reports to ensure that finances are in good order. Nothing undermines the confidence of the local community more than financial ineptitude by school administrators or school board members.

Effective school boards also take advantage of training programs provided by state school board associations. These programs are particularly useful to newly elected board members. Such programs familiarize them with their new responsibilities more quickly than relying solely on their local experiences. In most states these programs are inexpensive and are typically held in the evening at several convenient locations throughout a state.

A board president leading an effective school board will select members for the negotiating committee who will avoid making counterproductive remarks. Board negotiators need a thick skin and infinite patience. Local teacher negotiators, and more often regional representatives from the state teachers union, sometimes intentionally try to goad board members into making imprudent statements.

A teacher negotiating team will contain some members who have participated in negotiations for several previous contracts. Board members, on the other hand, typically have shorter tenures as board members and are often novices in the negotiations process. This puts school boards at a significant disadvantage in the bargaining process.

Good school board members recognize that the schools serve as a cohesive element in the community. Parents and students naturally take pride in their schools as a critical component of the community. This pride and cohesion often displays itself most prominently in support for the athletic teams fielded by the schools. Effective school board members, even if they personally are not avid fans of school athletics, recognize the critical role that such sports teams play in building cohesion in the community and support for the schools.

Citizens and board members with little interest in athletic programs sometimes resent the money and attention devoted to these activities. The cost of athletic and other extracurricular programs, including stipends paid to teacher coaches

and sponsors, consume only about 1 percent of the school budget. Extracurricular activities infuse students with future life and work skills such as working with
a team and subordinating their interests to those of the larger group.

Vibrant extracurricular and other after-school programs also keep middle
and high school students productively occupied in the after-school hours. This
is particularly important in a society where there are relatively few adults at
home or in the neighborhood in the hours between 3:00 p.m. and 6:00 p.m.

Of all the important characteristics of effective board members, having the
mind-set of a trustee may be the most important. Sometimes board members
enter board service thinking they were elected to represent only their own
views or those of a certain constituency or political subdivision. Board members actually have a trustee relationship toward students, citizens, and staff.
This means that a board member must promote the best interests of all of
these groups rather than narrowly focus on his or her own interests or those
of his or her core constituency.

Many school board members are elected from political subdivisions such
as townships or towns. This procedure actually reinforces the concept of representing a constituency rather than the interests of the whole school district.
A better procedure is electing officials "at large," which means that board
members are elected from the entire school community rather than a subdivision of it. In some states a local school board has a choice about whether or
not to hold elections on an "at-large" basis.

Board members must be careful about how they respond to requests from
citizens to take certain actions or represent parents' interests relative to school
personnel. Board members should encourage parents and citizens to first
follow the normal chain of command before involving themselves as board
members. If the parent or citizen is still not satisfied, the board member can
talk to the relevant school administrator, but not directly to a teacher, to get
a sense of the issue.

This should lead to remedial action by the school administrator, if appropriate, but a board member should attempt to force an issue only in rare circumstances. In some districts school board members may notice a pattern of indifference toward parental or citizen concerns. In that event, the superintendent
should be held accountable and should be expected to rectify the situation.

DYSFUNCTIONAL SCHOOL BOARDS

Most school superintendents who may work with fifty school board members
during their career would say that fewer than ten of these board members
were problematic in any way, and only a few were seriously disruptive to

the efficient and effective operation of the school district. Having said this, we must acknowledge that too many school districts are negatively impacted by the counterproductive behavior of their rogue school board members. As indicated in chapter 11, perhaps 25 percent of districts have dysfunctional school boards at any given time.

These dysfunctional school boards share similar characteristics. They have two or more members who tend to obsess over a few specific issues, have personality clashes with other board members or the superintendent, or have a narcissistic compulsion to be the center of attention. What are some of the characteristics of a dysfunctional school board? First and foremost is a lack of respect and honesty on the part of at least several board members. If one such member serves on a board, his or her negative influence can be contained. If there are two or more such people, however, they reinforce one another and can foment major disruptions in the efficient operation of the school district.

A few typical incidents involving superintendents illustrate this point. A superintendent once had an elementary principal who struck a teacher in the face in front of her class—a virtually unheard-of behavior. This male principal had exhibited some questionable behaviors toward his female teachers on other occasions. The superintendent successfully counseled this principal to resign from the district.

The night the resignation was to appear on the agenda, the superintendent met with the board in executive session to describe what had happened and the reason for the resignation. One board member objected to the resignation even though the district solicitor was present and assured the board that all proper legal precautions had been observed.

This board member raised some indirect objections to the resignation publicly, raising the curiosity of the media members at the meeting. Later that night he called the principal in question and advised him to sue the school district. The superintendent learned about this conversation because the principal contacted him the following morning to report that the board member had called him. Only the good sense of the former principal in question prevented a contentious legal issue over the resignation.

In some school districts, one or more board members are very indiscreet in e-mails or other communications with other board members, school officials, or parents. These communications are sometimes shared more widely in the community, often leading to controversies and confrontations at board meetings. Such controversies can take on a life of their own, leading to offended citizens demanding resignations of board members or school officials. It can take months for such incidents to fade from public discussion.

A third example concerns a board member who had an intense dislike for an assistant superintendent in the school district. On the monthly bill list at the public meeting he noticed that this administrator had submitted a mileage reimbursement request for attending a nearby conference. The board member objected to the payment, saying that he had attended that meeting, did not see the administrator in question, and that she therefore was lying about attending the meeting. Aside from the fact that the administrator in question was of the highest integrity, this breach of decorum and basic human decency elicited a heated response from the superintendent. None of this reflected well on the school board or administration.

These examples illustrate how a single individual on the school board can undermine the respect and confidence that a community would like to have in its public officials. These types of situations are minor, however, compared with cases in districts where a majority of the school board members act unethically and sometimes illegally. A recent case in Pennsylvania concerned a school superintendent in the last year of her contract. She was abruptly fired without cause by a five-to-four vote of the school board. This was a clear violation of her contract and will likely result in a judgment against the district of at least several hundred thousand dollars, in addition to significant legal fees.

All of this was in retaliation for the fact that most of these five board members had just lost a primary election for the next school board election. The community was disturbed by the antics of these board members in the recent past. Shortly thereafter this five-member majority conducted a questionable search for a new superintendent, freezing the remaining board members out of the planning process for the search. They also established a time line that was much too short to ensure that they would attract a suitable pool of candidates for the position.

Another school district had a school board president who handpicked his fellow board members because of their passivity and docility toward his illegal activities. He was able to do this by controlling the political party apparatus in the community and thus controlling who would be a candidate for school board. He was eventually convicted of illegal financial dealings between the school district and his private business. Such illegal behavior by board members is very unusual and yet its occurrence taints not only the school district involved but also all school boards and school administrators in the region.

One area in which even one or two rogue board members can do extensive harm is in labor relations. For forty years now, teachers in most states have had the right to negotiate contracts and secure a collective bargaining agreement. The states with the strongest unions and the most confrontational negotiation processes are generally along the east and west coasts of the United States and within the old industrial states of the Midwest.

Confrontational board members often lobby to have themselves appointed to the school board negotiating team and act as a disruptive influence during face-to-face negotiations with the union negotiating team. They often have an animus toward teachers and resent the salary levels and fringe benefits packages that many teachers enjoy.

One situation more than thirty-five years ago involved a superintendent attending his first negotiating session as a new superintendent in what was already a tense bargaining atmosphere. One board-member negotiator, who sent his children to private schools, told the teacher negotiators that they did not deserve a salary increase because they were too incompetent to teach students how to read. A teacher negotiator responded heatedly that teachers could do a better job of teaching reading if the community didn't send them so many stupid children. This anecdote was shared among the district's teachers and played a direct role in the teachers taking a strike vote one month later.

These examples are not unique; similar incidents occur in school districts and other public governance bodies around the country. The salient point is that such behavior by school board officials undermines the reputation of the school district and makes it more difficult to garner public support for the difficult decisions that school boards must make on a regular basis.

The time and attention that must be devoted to a constant stream of minor scandals and controversies in such dysfunctional school districts detracts from the attention that a school board can give to its core functions. As much as one-third of school board meeting time in such districts can be consumed by issues that really have little to do with educating students or operating an effective organization.

We can postulate a corollary to Gresham's Law—that "bad money drives out good"—by observing that in dysfunctional school districts bad school board members drive out good members. In such districts reasonable and conscientious board members decline to run for an additional term, or even resign in midterm rather than subject themselves to interacting with several contentious fellow board members. Districts with a well-deserved poor reputation then find it difficult to recruit reasonable candidates for board positions, raising the likelihood that additional contentious people will form the pool of candidates for future elections.

School boards whose meetings resemble a three-ring circus have a devastating effect on morale within the district. The knowledge that your designated leaders act like buffoons undermines the positive level of employee job satisfaction that is a hallmark of a healthy and effective school district. School administrators whose very jobs and reputations are held hostage by the actions of such a school board suffer this demoralization with particular force.

A VIEWER'S GUIDE TO A SCHOOL BOARD MEETING

The relatively recent phenomenon of broadcasting school board meetings on local cable channels has greatly increased the audience for these public meetings. Heretofore, only a handful of citizens and one or two members of the press attended school board meetings. The following is a guide to what to look for while watching a school board meeting. First of all, relatively boring meetings are good from a governance standpoint if not from an entertainment perspective. A smoothly running meeting reflects good planning by the superintendent and the board president in preparing the agenda for the meeting.

A well-designed agenda contains mostly routine items as well as a few items requiring board discussion. Board members should have sufficient familiarity with the routine items so that they are able to act intelligently upon the superintendent's recommendation. Ideally, an item is not listed for action unless and until the superintendent or his subordinates have provided the board members a sufficient rationale to approve the recommendation.

Sometimes a topic must be addressed before the board has reached a consensus on the proper course of action. These are the situations where board members interact with one another and the superintendent to discuss the topic in question. These opportunities can provide excellent examples of democracy in action since citizens can observe the deliberative process in real time. It is good practice to have one or two such discussions at every school board meeting. This gives the community confidence in their elected board and avoids the misperception that all decisions are made behind closed doors.

Most decisions by the board are a result of discussions at previous meetings or of meetings of committees of the board. Those who only attend the regular board meeting do not know about the prior consideration of a topic. This often leads the casual observer to mistakenly conclude that the board is simply rubber-stamping the recommendations of the superintendent.

A school board meeting is technically a meeting of the board held in "public." It is not a "public meeting" in the normal sense of the term. The chairman of the board should preside over the school board meeting. She should follow normal parliamentary procedures in considering each motion for board action. The superintendent usually has a place on the agenda for her report and may speak from time to time on agenda items as requested, or as she deems necessary.

The superintendent should be careful not to monopolize discussions or inject herself or himself too often into discussions. This is a meeting for the board of directors and should not be controlled by the superintendent. A superintendent should not, however, be so passive that she or he seldom participates in the meeting.

A sure sign of a dysfunctional board is when one or two board members become argumentative with their colleagues or are obviously trying to sabotage the smooth consideration of school board business. Some board members go so far as to personally attack their board colleagues or the superintendent. They may also make more generic attacks on the school district or specific schools.

They sometimes make attacks on individual staff members. Such virulent attacks, while clearly wrong on their face, also present potential legal problems for the school district. This is because rank-and-file staff members are not public figures and cannot be attacked publicly without risking possible legal challenge.

Board meetings may range in length from twenty-five minutes to seven hours. Both extremes are undesirable. A very short meeting allows no time for board interaction or for comments and concerns from the public to be addressed. A seven-hour board meeting, on the other hand, is about five hours too long.

One such board meeting included a five-hour discussion about what type of surface, real grass or artificial grass, should be approved for athletic fields on a new middle school campus. More than thirty citizens expressed their opinion on the issue, often in a very heated and confrontational manner. A couple of board members added fuel to the fire and further polarized both the school board and the community. Such meetings are no doubt highly entertaining, but they are also highly destructive to effective school governance.

Meetings lasting about two hours seem to be about right. There is time to conduct the regular business of the board, for board members to interact, to feature one or two elements of the school program, and to provide an opportunity for comments from citizens. Another reason for meetings of reasonable length is the recognition that most board members and visitors have day jobs and long evening meetings can cause fatigue. Fatigue leads to poor-quality thinking and often to testiness among the participants.

Every school district seems to have three to five people who attend every school board meeting and exhibit a consistently adversarial attitude toward the school district. Their most frequent complaints concern the deficiencies of the staff, the failure of the board to meet its obligations, and the perennial displeasure about rising school costs.

There once was a seventy-seven-year-old man who complained weekly in his column in the local newspaper about the proposal that an elementary school should be closed and replaced on another site. He consistently talked about how the facility in question was totally adequate. He was finally invited to visit this school to see for himself the condition of the facility. He quickly recognized the deteriorating condition of the school. He was asked when he had last been inside the school. He said that he last visited when he was seventeen—which was sixty years before.

Another constant attendee in the same district attacked the superintendent on a monthly basis. These attacks by a person who had never spoken with or met the superintendent outside the board meeting continued for about six months. The superintendent called the gentleman and asked him about his issue. The gentleman said that the superintendent should not take his criticism personally. Ten years before he had called the previous superintendent to complain about his daughter's grade on an algebra test. The superintendent refused to change the grade. The man said that ever since that incident, he has had no time for school superintendents.

A constant visitor in another school district took full advantage of the age of televised board meetings. Whenever he rose to address the school board, he didn't direct his remarks to board members but rather looked directly into the TV camera. This person used every opportunity to broadcast his critical views of the district and school board to the wider community.

Frequently there are contingents of parents, students, or staff who come to a board meeting to plead their case for more resources for their school, their athletic team, or other collective endeavor. These folks are invariably polite and present their petitions in a respectful manner. In well-run school board meetings, board members or the superintendent may make brief remarks to the speakers. The board president often asks the superintendent to investigate the concern and resolve the concern or bring it back to the board for further discussion. It is poor practice to become argumentative with citizen speakers, particularly with those who are trying to create a scene at the meeting.

The importance of well-conducted board meetings is paramount in crafting favorable public opinion about the school district. This is, after all, the only venue in which the community can observe its elected leaders in action. Unfortunately, a spate of dysfunctional board meetings makes a vivid impression that can take years to overcome. It is a major task of the superintendent and the board president to ensure that school board meetings are conducted efficiently and effectively.

In chapter 11, "The Limits of Local Control," readers may have formed the impression that school board members are not really critical to the operation of a school district. This is not the case. The many examples of good and bad behavior by board members in this chapter demonstrate that board members can and do have an important impact on the operations of a school district.

Boards set a tone and climate in a school district that can significantly impact the effectiveness of a district. They engender trust among board members, the leadership team, and the general community. Positive school board behavior has a compounding effect over time, yielding the maximum benefit in district reputation and performance within a five-year period. A poorly performing board, on the other hand, can have a serious negative impact on school operations and reputation in less than a year that often can take years to remediate.

13

The Superintendent—CEO of the School District

The superintendent of schools is the equivalent of the CEO of a business enterprise. He is responsible for the day-to-day operation of the schools and is the chief agent of the board of directors. The board is charged with setting policy for the school district while the superintendent is charged with implementing the policy. Most importantly, an effective superintendent provides vision and goals for the district and inspires both the staff and the community to pursue excellence in the school system.

The superintendent is the chief advisor to the board and recommends major changes in policy and practices of the district for school board approval. He is the top administrative officer in the school district and is responsible for the actions of all school district employees that he monitors through the selection, evaluation, and placement of all personnel.

The school superintendency as such has existed for little more than one hundred years. In colonial times and the first century of our republic, school boards hired personnel directly and there were no administrative officials between the school board and its teachers. The first administrative position to become common was that of head teacher, a position that slowly evolved into that of principal.

As districts became larger and more complex, school boards began to hire the predecessors of what would become known as *school superintendents.* During this same period in the late nineteenth century, state legislatures became very active in formulating school attendance regulations and in contributing to the financing of the schools. States began to mandate that districts create high schools as well as the elementary schools that had been required for some time.

In the nineteenth century it was impossible to closely supervise the operation of the schools from the state capital because of transportation and communications limitations. To remedy this problem, states created a position most frequently known as a *supervising principal.* This official was the equivalent of a circuit rider who visited schools within a geographic area, usually at the county level.

The office at this time was mainly clerical because these supervising principals were not in any one jurisdiction long enough to implement effective supervision and direction. It wasn't until the early decades of the twentieth century that the school superintendency as we now know it came into being.

As states came to require more information about district operations and began to finance a larger portion of the school budget, they also established eligibility standards for school superintendents. School superintendents are answerable to the state department of education in myriad ways and forms. They are responsible for carrying out state laws and regulations passed by the legislature and the department of education. They must authenticate a plethora of state reports, particularly as they relate to school finances.

In most states school superintendents are actually state officials appointed locally. In many states, superintendents take the same oath of office, often before a judge, as do the governor and legislators of a state. In most states these eligibility requirements include both educational and experience elements. To become a school superintendent one needs to pursue graduate-level courses in educational administration. The candidate must also have at least several years of teaching experience and prior administrative experience, usually as a building principal. These regulations are now being waived in some states, especially for large urban districts.

The country's fourteen thousand school superintendents are overwhelmingly white with a large majority being male. In recent decades, however, woman superintendents have become increasingly common. Today about one-fourth of school superintendents are female. The average age for school superintendents is just under fifty and their average salary is about $125,000 per year. Salaries range from less than $100,000 in smaller rural districts to well over $300,000 in the nation's largest or most affluent school districts.

The nation's twenty-five largest school districts are much more likely to have minority and women superintendents than school districts as a whole. The average tenure of a school superintendent is approximately four years. In large urban districts the average tenure is less than three years. It is sometimes said in jest that school superintendents are the country's highest paid migrant workers.

Few if any high school or college graduates enter adulthood with the thought of becoming a school superintendent. New teachers concentrate on mastering teaching, a task that requires at least several years. Only then do a small percentage of teachers begin to entertain the thought of becoming a school principal. This step requires additional education, including a master's degree, and typically requires several years of part-time study before securing the necessary credentials.

The first step on the administrative ladder, at least at the secondary level, is to serve as an assistant principal at a middle school or high school. Several years as a subordinate administrator in an assistant position can then lead to selection as a middle or high school principal. Elementary teachers often take leadership positions such as grade level chairs prior to becoming an elementary school principal.

It is from the principal's perspective that the new administrator begins to interact with central office personnel including the superintendent. Principals acquire a sense of what the top job might entail and may then begin additional graduate work, requiring several more years of study, to earn the credentials necessary to pursue a superintendency.

In most cases an aspiring superintendent will first serve in a subordinate central office position such as assistant superintendent for instruction, human resources director, or business administrator. Only then will the future superintendent have the necessary background and experience to be a serious contender for a superintendency in all but the smallest districts. By this time, our fledgling superintendent is forty-five to fifty years old, usually with half-grown children and a spouse with his or her own well-established career.

A midcareer professional with the family circumstances described here typically has limited mobility. He or she is likely to apply for superintendent positions within a restricted geographic area. This not only limits the opportunities available to any one administrator but also diminishes the number of applications that a school district will likely receive for an open position. There has been a precipitous decline in the number of applicants for open superintendent positions in recent decades, partly because of the mobility issue. This was less of an issue two generations ago when the superintendent candidate, almost always a male, would have a "trailing" spouse who did not have a career outside the home.

Another major factor limiting the number of applicants is that the position itself has simply become more complex and precarious over the last forty years. In most states a principal retains at least limited tenure rights, if not as a principal, at least as a teacher. This job security is sacrificed as one enters the superintendency, a position with notoriously low job security. School districts seeking a superintendent in the 1970s often had fifty or more applicants for the position. In more recent superintendent searches, the applicant pool has declined precipitously.

MAJOR FUNCTIONS
OF THE SUPERINTENDENT

The six major tasks of a superintendent as CEO involve the personnel function, finance and budgeting, curriculum and instruction, school facilities and
operations, community relations, and effective interaction with the school
board. The most critical factor to a superintendent's success is working productively with the school board. Most superintendents who lose their jobs do
so because of disagreements with their school board.

A major cause of disagreements with the school board concern superintendents who attempt to be too directive with a board in areas that are of critical interest to board members as representatives of the community. While a
superintendent should be fairly assertive about recommendations involving
the educational program, matters directly impacting taxes and public opinion
should be discussed more fully with the school board.

In matters of this type it is good practice to provide the board with three
alternative approaches to an issue. Ample background research should also be
provided so that they understand the implications of each alternative. Armed
with this information, board members would discuss the issues among themselves and arrive at a consensus as to the best course of action. While tensions
between the board and superintendent are often the fault of the superintendent, just as often the problem lies with a few challenging board members, as
discussed previously.

While interactions with the school board are the most significant factor in
a superintendent's immediate success, the superintendent's long-term effect
on a school district involves the quality of school personnel that the district
attracts and retains. A strategy to improve the overall quality of personnel in
a school district is by its nature a long-term project. It involves the selection
process, training programs to improve teaching, teacher evaluation processes,
compensation policies, and the climate and morale within the schools. The
same nurturing and developmental approach needs to be taken with administrative personnel as with the teaching force.

The personnel selection process raises the issue of nepotism. Public employment in many jurisdictions is viewed as a privilege to be dispensed by
politicians and public administrators to their friends and supporters. This
practice finds its way into many school districts. While the hiring of support
staff based partly on personal connections is not ideal, it really doesn't have
much effect on the educational process. The employment of teachers and
administrators, on the other hand, directly affects instruction and should not
be tainted by even the hint of nepotism.

A good superintendent resists the inevitable efforts by community members, staff, and board members to influence the hiring process. The superintendent should stand firm in insisting on the integrity of the process. This will not win many friends for the superintendent. There is an old saying that when ten applicants are interviewed for a position, the interviewer ends up with nine enemies and one ingrate.

While changes in personnel practices will become apparent to school staff in short order, the effects of improved personnel policies and procedures may not be apparent to the general community for years, if at all. The likelihood that school board members and the wider community will perceive a connection between improvement in the quality of personnel over time and the resulting positive impact on the educational program is unlikely.

The staff and community might perceive an improvement in the school district over time, but they will not attribute this to personnel policies or to the superintendent who implemented them. In other words, this approach to improving the school district will have high impact but low visibility.

School finance and budgeting is the aspect of a superintendent's work that is usually most apparent to the school board, staff, and community. While a superintendent can influence a school district to operate more efficiently and can rally support from the board and community for expensive improvements, these effects only minimally impact school costs over the long term. A superintendent who implements spending efficiencies over time can influence the overall school budget by a few percentage points. This is usually desirable but hardly a significant change.

A school superintendent has very little influence over the revenue side of a budget. Other than by influencing tax rates and thus real estate taxes, a superintendent is subject to the vagaries of state funding formulas and the regional and national economy. If the country is in a recession, the school district will see declines in earned income tax revenues, declines in transfer taxes from home sales, and more modest increases in state funding. If interest rates decline, the district will earn less from investing tax funds short term until they are needed, a not insignificant impact on school revenue.

On the expense side of the budget, there are a few significant costs that increase greatly but are not directly related to the educational process. The most significant of these is the escalating cost of health insurance. Decades ago these costs were only a small percentage of a school budget—hence the term *fringe benefits.* Today they may constitute up to 15 percent of the budget and they represent an increasing proportion of expenses with each passing year. There are also employer-mandatory taxes relating to salary such as Social Security and pension contributions. These two items require an additional expenditure of more than 10 percent above base salary increases.

The other escalating expense, not related to education, is the increasing energy costs over the past several decades. A great deal of money is necessary for fuel for the buses and for lighting, heating, and cooling of the schools. Once a school district takes reasonable steps to conserve energy, there is not much more a district can do to counteract increasing energy costs. These costs can consume more than 3 percent of the school budget.

The largest area of the budget is personnel costs. As discussed elsewhere, a district really has little control over salary levels in the long term. A review of average teacher salaries over the past forty years reveals that they closely track the inflation rate over the same period. The one place that personnel costs can be controlled relates to the number of teachers and other staff members. The superintendent is constantly under pressure from the staff and parents to add staff to initiate new programs or to decrease overall class size in the district.

Because of these ongoing pressures, there is a tendency in most districts for staffing levels to increase incrementally over time. Reversing this trend in bad economic times is one option open to a superintendent and school board. Unfortunately for the superintendent, reducing staff is highly unpopular with everyone except those concerned about tax rates. A superintendent makes ten enemies for every friend in a staff-reduction scenario.

A superintendent's influence on curriculum and instruction, although often indirect, can be significant. In the absence of state-mandated curricula, the district must ensure that teachers develop rigorous curricula. If state-mandated curricula are in place, the district must ensure that each curriculum area is faithfully taught. Without the superintendent insisting on a rigorous monitoring regimen, some teachers will not follow curriculum guidelines. This monitoring can be accomplished through the teacher supervision process, ensuring that the curriculum is taught through an appropriate instructional plan.

The superintendent's role is to ensure that a rigorous curriculum is in fact developed and then, through the teacher supervision process, ensure that the curriculum is taught through an appropriate instructional plan. The burden for monitoring the curriculum in most school districts, however, falls on the building administrator. Unfortunately, administrative staffing levels in most districts are such that the building administrator does not have the time necessary to perform this task in a satisfactory manner.

A previous chapter indicated that curriculum decisions at the local level are constrained by regulations and guidelines mandated by the state. Thus local curriculum development must operate within the constraints and parameters allowed by the state regulations.

The other factor limiting local curriculum development is the textbooks that are available to support a given curriculum. As mentioned elsewhere, textbook treatment of many subjects is less than optimal due to the influence of pressure groups on state textbook selection committees in large states such as Texas and California. These textbooks, often eviscerated of challenging content because of political correctness, become the only ones available to states and school districts nationwide.

While a superintendent has overall responsibility for school facilities and operations, his involvement is usually indirect through the office of the business administrator. The superintendent's role takes a much higher profile when a school district must seek bond issue approvals for major school renovations or the construction of new buildings.

Such construction projects often have implications far beyond the simple financing of the projects. New or renovated buildings cause internal dissension among different departments in the schools who are competing for new facilities or the renovation of existing facilities. New or renovated facilities often have repercussions involving grade levels housed in the facilities as well as changes in attendance boundaries within a district. Both of these issues engage the attention of parents, taxpayers, and staff members.

These issues can often be highly contentious and can adversely affect the political standing of both the superintendent and the school board. Thus, while facilities are usually a back-burner issue for a superintendent, they can engender major controversies once new construction or major renovation projects come to the fore.

A superintendent's role in community relations is one of his most important and visible responsibilities. The main forum for displaying the public persona of the superintendent is at school board meetings. This is even more salient today as many school districts televise their school board meetings, making them available to a wider audience. Heretofore, the main mechanism for citizens to evaluate a superintendent was through reports from school board meetings in the local press. Today, projecting a good media presence is yet an additional challenge for the superintendent.

A superintendent of schools has a critical ceremonial role in the district. In this sense, the superintendent, like the president of the United States, is a head of state as well as the chief executive of the organization. An effective superintendent performs this ceremonial role by being highly visible at local school events. He or she attends football games, high school plays, middle school band concerts, and elementary school back-to-school nights.

The superintendent has no formal role in these proceedings, but simply shows his or her interest in the day-to-day activities of the students and teachers. He or she should also be a member of local service groups such as the

Lions Club and be available to be a speaker at community meetings. He or she is also an occasional speaker at parent-teacher events. In these venues, the superintendent has an opportunity to take the pulse of parents and influential citizens regarding current issues and public attitudes toward the school district.

These ceremonial and functional events require that a conscientious superintendent attend from 100 to 120 evening events in the course of a school year. About thirty to forty of these events involve the school board, while the rest are attendance at the types of school activities listed previously. A superintendent who fails to attend to these ceremonial activities pays a high price in community support and regard. Attention to these community-relations opportunities is a critical factor in the long-term success of a superintendent.

During the school year, a superintendent is involved in evening meetings about three nights per week. Performing his ceremonial role by attending school-level functions also consumes at least parts of many weekends during the year. A superintendent who keeps regular work hours during the normal workweek will thus spend fifty-five to sixty hours per week in job-related activities.

A normal workweek for a superintendent involves many internal planning meetings with his or her immediate subordinates, as well as individual meetings with the top lieutenants to discuss timely issues. She or he will likely attend one or more community service meetings and may well address staff or parent-teacher groups about current school district issues. Much behind-the-scenes work is done to prepare for and follow up on school board meetings.

Attending meetings at the county level to coordinate countywide educational services in areas such as special education and technical education will also occur once or twice a month. At any given time, the superintendent also will need to become involved in the more complex and difficult personnel issues facing the district.

A good superintendent is also out and about visiting the several schools in the district. She or he should take these opportunities to talk with administrators and teachers on their own turf about topics of concern to them. This also provides the superintendent with an informal way to evaluate the quality of the educational program in the schools. He or she will probably spend one or two hours a day on correspondence, e-mails, and phone calls. His most frequent contacts will be with other district administrators, union leaders, and school board members.

SUPERINTENDENT-BOARD RELATIONS

As mentioned previously, the most critical factor to the success of a superintendent is his or her relationship with the school board. The school board looks to the superintendent as its chief advisor on educational matters. A new superintendent must earn the trust of the school board over the first several months of his or her tenure. To earn this trust the superintendent must exhibit the highest level of honesty and integrity. If school board members perceive that their superintendent shades the truth or lacks integrity in any sense, it is only a matter of time before the superintendent loses board support and is dismissed, or at the very least does not have his contract renewed.

The most important tests of a superintendent's integrity involve taking responsibility for the inevitable mistakes that she or he makes as well as admitting to the inevitable misguided actions of school staff. In this regard, a superintendent is well advised to take the counterintuitive step of sharing bad news with the school board sooner rather than later.

It is a natural human reaction in the face of bad news to try to ignore it and hope to somehow correct the problem before it becomes public knowledge. This is possible regarding some minor issues, but the superintendent cannot ignore obvious and irremediable problems. She or he should make the school board aware of the problem and also provide some guidance as to the options available to the board for remediating serious deficiencies. Aggressive laws in many states regarding the public's "right to know" place constraints on the issues that a superintendent can discuss with a school board outside a formal meeting. These legal requirements tend to diminish communications between the school board and the superintendent.

A major element in building trust with board members is to treat each of them with respect and equity. A superintendent receives many questions and requests from individual board members outside the context of school board meetings. He needs to decide in each case whether the issue in question is specific to the single board member or whether it might have wider implications for the district or the school board.

If the issue is of wider potential significance, it should be shared with the entire board via the normal periodic written communications sent to all board members. Most superintendents communicate with board members regularly. Superintendents do, however, need to be extremely careful in what they put into writing, particularly in e-mails to board members. Today, e-mails are subject to the discovery process in lawsuits involving a school district.

Another way that a superintendent shows respect is in the manner in which he or she deals with the inevitable personnel problems that must be brought to the board's attention. A school board expects the superintendent to be a manager with high expectations for his staff. The board also expects the superintendent to be fair-minded and to treat his subordinates well.

School staff members expect the superintendent to protect them from unfair criticism from the board, parents, and the community. It is sometimes difficult to satisfy all of these expectations. The superintendent should take every opportunity to present staff members in a positive light to the school board. He or she also should take opportunities to present a positive view of the school board to staff members. Both of these initiatives promote cohesion between a school board and the school staff.

In recent years most states have passed "Right to Know" laws of varying strictness regarding the types of communications, reports, and other documents that are available for public scrutiny. This is another development that has made the job of superintendents and school board members more difficult. There are always matters that a superintendent would like to discuss with a school board, but will decline to do so if the discussion will be available to the public.

This dynamic actually retards the level of information available to school board members in the performance of their duties. The constraints placed on communication between the superintendent and the school board over the past several decades have increased dramatically, to the detriment of effective school governance.

A superintendent working with a dysfunctional school board has an added communications problem. On such boards one or two members may feel free to break the confidentiality that should exist among the school board members and the superintendent. These members will freely share confidential communications in an effort to undermine the superintendent or other members of the board. Such a breach of trust has a corrosive effect on superintendent–school board relations. Furthermore, such behavior greatly encumbers the level of communication between a superintendent and his board of directors.

This lack of respect and basic decency by a few board members is the hallmark of a dysfunctional school board. Even two such members on a board can seriously affect school governance. It requires exceptional political and interpersonal skills on the part of the superintendent and school board presidents to navigate a productive course for the district under such conditions.

Integrity and honesty on the part of the superintendent are necessary, but not sufficient, to his or her success. She or he must also be competent and conscientious in the performance of the superintendent's duties. The superintendent should also serve as a role model in his or her personal life and activities. Demonstrated competence will gain support from members of the staff and community, even among those who do not particularly care for him or her at a personal level.

Unfortunately, too many superintendents lose their position even if they exhibit the highest personal and professional standards. These are superintendents who have the misfortune to serve a dysfunctional school board and find themselves involved in a political controversy to which there is no good solution. In that event, the superintendent can become the scapegoat for the toxic political environment in a particular community. Many superintendents find themselves in such untenable situations either because of dysfunctional boards or intractable political environments.

THE EFFECTIVE SUPERINTENDENT

We have briefly reviewed the major categories where a superintendent needs to exercise strong leadership. What is leadership in the context of the school superintendency? Business theorists on leadership often speak of transformational and transactional leadership. A *transformational leader* is one who takes a school district in a dramatically new direction or who inspires his staff to dramatically higher levels of performance. A *transactional leader* is one whose main efforts are concentrated on maintaining and fine-tuning the existing organization.

It should be obvious from the litany of constraints that schools are subject to that transformational leadership is very hard to accomplish in a public bureaucracy such as a local school system. A minority of superintendents can succeed in the effort, but it is a long and difficult road. The transformation usually takes so long that the community and staff do not consciously realize the magnitude of the change that has evolved. Nonetheless, it is gratifying that a fair number of visionary and dynamic leaders are able to successfully lead school districts throughout the nation.

Most school districts are of such a small size that the superintendent does not have the luxury of delegating all routine business to subordinates while she or he concentrates on major initiatives. Such delegation may work at large corporations, major universities, and hospitals, but can seldom be implemented at the local school district level.

A school superintendent can more accurately be compared to the owner or CEO of a middle-sized company, perhaps with several hundred employees. He or she must become personally involved in the daily maintenance tasks common to any human enterprise. It is useful to think of any organization as being characterized by the physics concept known as *entropy*. This is the tendency in nature for all things to deteriorate and disaggregate over time. The manager's transactional task is to constantly perform maintenance tasks and make small adjustments to make certain that the organization continues to function well. These are the activities that require the lion's share of a superintendent's time and effort.

Typical examples of such maintenance activities include filling vacant positions, ordering and receiving supplies and materials, supervising and evaluating subordinate personnel, responding to community and parental complaints, and interacting with school board members in a responsive manner. Maintenance functions also include constantly recurring minor emergencies and incidents that interfere with the smooth operation of a school district.

One superintendent experienced an incident where a high school student left a bomb threat on the door of a chemistry classroom. This threatening message was discovered first thing in the morning. The principal followed proper procedure by evacuating the school and requesting assistance from the police department.

Many of the 1,200 students in the high school began calling their parents on their cell phones, sharing rumors that soon spread to the wider community. Within twenty minutes a helicopter from a local TV station was flying over the school campus and broadcasting pictures of the high school student body rapidly dispersing over the football field.

The superintendent's office immediately began receiving phone calls from parents, community members and the press demanding to know what was going on. At this point, of course, the superintendent had no idea what was going on. The next few hours were spent seeking accurate information about the bomb threat, developing a response to the media, and communicating the facts to the community.

The district actually did a fairly good job of handling the situation. There were plenty of Monday morning quarterbacks, however, who spent the next few weeks speculating about what should be done to improve the reaction to such an event in the future. One student issuing a threat that had no foundation was thus able to disrupt an entire high school for half a day and produce a public relations problem for the district.

Another all-too-common example of events that can disrupt the smooth operation of the schools are reports of potential sexual predators stalking students at bus stops. When this occurs, the local media report unsubstantiated rumors that serve to traumatize parents. This leads to scores of calls from anxious parents demanding that the alleged stalker be captured.

Before long the superintendent finds himself giving interviews to TV stations and trying to implement existing procedure that will protect students. As often as not, the threat disappears without incident and after a few days the district returns to normal. In the meantime these types of crises, real or imagined, distract the district leadership from its regular tasks.

These incidents point to a reality in school district administration that is far less common in private businesses or in other public entities. School district operations are more visible to the general public and parents than are those of other organizations. Superintendents who have the opportunity to serve as CEO of a small, private business or as a member of the board of trustees of a major community hospital or a major university will testify to the dramatic differences between public and private administration.

Experience as a CEO of a small, private business presents the greatest contrast between managing a private versus a public entity. Small, private businesses need only to be concerned with their own survival and profitability. Management challenges are limited to internal issues involving management of personnel and resources. Policies and major initiatives could be discussed and approved by the board of directors with no concern about the public reaction or adverse commentary in the media. The CEO could be confident that all board members were motivated by the hope that the enterprise would success.

This is not always the case with school board members, some of whom seek election to purposely frustrate the efforts of the school district or the superintendent. When the board of directors of a private company makes a decision, it can be carried out almost immediately. There is no need to garner support from the general public or to gain the acquiescence of various employee groups.

Newspapers do not report on the effectiveness of the private organization nor do people typically write letters to the editor attacking the practices or personnel of the private enterprise. Staff members did not privately lobby their friends and neighbors to thwart or change initiatives of the board of directors of the corporation. Such subtle undermining of school district initiative is an all-too-common occurrence.

An interesting incident occurred on a community hospital board where it became necessary for the board to hold one of its meetings in public. This was a consequence of a new requirement of a hospital accreditation agency that hospitals hold periodic public meetings as a part of the accreditation process.

The hospital was having a dispute with neighbors at the time about a possible expansion of hospital facilities that would have an impact on the neighborhood. The hospital board was positively petrified at the prospect of holding a meeting publicly and being subjected to unwelcome questions and challenges from members of the community.

Several of these board members were themselves top executives in major corporations. They served on several private and community boards but were very apprehensive about conducting a public meeting. Needless to say, such public scrutiny is a regular element of serving on a school board or of being the superintendent of the school district.

Managers in the private sector are often critical of public officials by pointing out that private corporations must meet a payroll and satisfy their customers or they will go out of business. Critics say that schools, on the other hand, have a captive audience and secure their funding through taxation. This observation is certainly accurate. A critical difference, however, is that in the private sector, customers voluntarily do business with the organization.

With the schools, however, 75 percent of the public does not have an immediate and obvious stake in the schools. This makes raising tax rates to support the schools a difficult sell to the general public. Those who have worked in both environments find that serving as a CEO in a public school district is far more challenging than a similar job in the private sector.

The factors discussed here make the school superintendency a precarious position. Working with ever-changing school boards, buffeted by events external to the schools, and subject to internal strains that can easily spill over into public controversies, the superintendent has little job security. Superintendents in most states do not have tenure and thus a continuing right to their position.

Most superintendents have an employment contract of from three to five years that provides some protection against improper removal from their position. This provides the superintendent time and opportunity to bring about needed changes in the district while supplying some level of stability to leadership in the district.

In the last year of a contract, a superintendent is essentially an "at-will" employee who may simply fail to have his contract renewed by the school board. A board may remove a superintendent at any point in the contract for cause, which may need to be adjudicated in the courts. Such legal niceties, however, do not prevent a dysfunctional school board from dismissing a superintendent in midterm without proper cause. This scenario causes extreme consternation in a school community and is counterproductive in every sense.

The school superintendency is an important and challenging career. To perform the job successfully requires the highest level of experience, judgment, interpersonal skills, and integrity. It is a high-stakes position that can potentially yield great rewards for the students and staff. Perhaps the best advice for an aspiring superintendent can be encapsulated in the words of a former superintendent. He offered three pieces of advice for a new superintendent: (1) always tell the truth, (2) never lose your sense of humor, and (3) always be ready and willing to lose your job.

14

The Critical Role of the School Principal

There are about one hundred thousand individual schools in the United States. All but the very smallest are under the direction of the school principal. The person most critical to improving student achievement is the school principal. The factor that most significantly influences the success of a principal, aside from her or his own talents and skills, is the context in which the school operates.

Even the most competent and inspirational principal cannot succeed in a fractured community with a mediocre and dispirited faculty. An otherwise ordinary principal, on the other hand, can successfully lead a school where students are eager learners and faculty members are both competent and engaged. Truly excellent schools, however, invariably have excellent principals.

In most school districts, the principal is the equivalent of a first-level supervisor in the private sector. He or she has risen from the teaching profession to the position of school principal. The typical elementary principal supervises about twenty to thirty staff members in a school of about three hundred to five hundred students. Middle schools typically have six hundred to eight hundred students and a staff of fifty or more. High schools range in size from one hundred students to more than three thousand students. Thus high school staffs can range from ten to over two hundred.

As a first-level supervisor, the school principal is a classic middle manager. He or she must spend a large proportion of time dealing with the personalities and conflicts of the school staff. This is the common fate of all middle managers. The principal's workday consists of a series of unrelated incidents and quick decisions on a myriad of issues. Most principals will testify that on many occasions their day is so hectic that the countless incidents that consume the day begin to run together as the day progresses.

One difference between a typical middle manager and a school principal is that the principal is not simply dealing with twenty to fifty adults in a self-contained environment. The principal must cope with personality and conflict issues involving hundreds, if not thousands, of students as well as the concerns of many parents. Any untoward event involving the school also quickly becomes grist for the media mill.

The true dimension of the difficulties of these interactions with faculty, students, and parents can be demonstrated in the context of the level of mental stability of the general population. A National Institute of Mental Health study in 2008 found that 26 percent of American adults suffer from a diagnosable mental disorder in any given year (National Institute of Mental Health, 2006, 1). Even assuming that only a small percentage of this number suffer from serious disorders, a principal of a 1,200-student high school may be dealing with a handful of unstable staff members, scores of mentally troubled students, and more than one hundred parents with mental disorders. This large number of psychologically fragile individuals presents the principal with a steady stream of school-related problems and conflicts.

Even thirty-five years ago unstable students were a recurring problem even in an affluent suburban high school. One day the secretary rushed into a principal's office and anxiously told him that there was a student in the outer office holding a gun who demanded to see him. The principal responded by asking, "Does he have an appointment?" The gunman overheard this rather insouciant remark, became rattled, and immediately ran from the building. He was soon apprehended and arrested by the local police. A high school principal, working daily with thousands of adolescents, often feels that he or she sits atop a powder keg liable to explode at any moment.

Most principals attain their first position between the ages of thirty-five and forty-five. They are often selected for a variety of perceived talents ranging from organizational abilities, to good interpersonal relations skills, to instructional expertise. Less than one quarter of principals rise to a higher rung on the administrative ladder and most spend the second half of their educational career at the principalship level.

A disproportionate number of administrators at the secondary level are former athletic coaches as well as classroom teachers. By virtue of serving as athletic coaches, these educators have an opportunity to display their leadership abilities as well as their ability to motivate and inspire young people. They also tend to be better known throughout the community than a typical teacher because of their involvement with athletics.

When superintendents, school boards, teachers, and parents consider the characteristics of a good principal, instructional expertise is not usually among their top concerns. The school community typically seeks someone who can manage the school efficiently and can deal effectively with students and teachers.

The ideal principal from a teacher's perspective is one who supports the teachers in their inevitable conflicts with students and parents, maintains a well-ordered learning environment, and only minimally monitors curriculum and classroom activities. A loose-supervision model is the ideal from a teacher's viewpoint. A superintendent and school board seek the same management qualities as do teachers and parents, but they also seek good community-relations skills and a collaborative and supportive attitude toward advancing district-level initiatives. Prudence and good judgment are also highly valued by the upper levels of administration and the school board.

The management tasks of principals primarily include the organization of classes, the assignment of teachers, and the utilization of physical spaces. This is more important educationally than many people realize. A high school principal in a school of 1,200 students, for example, develops a master schedule that determines how 1,200 students and perhaps 80 teachers will spend one thousand hours during the school year.

Each year principals must also allocate limited school instructional budgets for textbooks and supplies. Should the principal buy new math books for geometry classes or new microscopes for one of the biology labs? The decisions over a five-year period significantly influence the quality of the instructional program in a school.

The most significant impact on the quality of an instructional program, however, is the quality of the teaching staff. Personnel selection procedures and supervision practices significantly impact instructional quality and thus student achievement. The level of involvement of principals in teacher selection ranges among districts from no involvement to total involvement.

Lack of involvement in teacher selection is most commonly found in urban school districts with large personnel departments. Such departments usually have major concerns about staff diversity and dealing with cumbersome teachers union contract requirements regarding the assignment of new teachers. In these urban environments, teachers with experience in poorly performing schools often have the right to be reassigned to more successful and desirable schools as openings occur. Principals often have nothing to say about a teacher being transferred from their building or another teacher being assigned to their school.

While acknowledging the validity of an experienced teacher wanting to transfer from a troubled school to a more congenial teaching environment, the impact on the principal as instructional leader can be devastating. A valid principle of supervisory theory holds that a supervisor with a role in selecting her staff will have a vested interest in the new teacher's success and will work hard to validate her selection decision. This motivator is lacking in districts where principals have little or no control over teacher selection.

The more typical scenario is for the principal to have an integral role in the teacher selection process. She or he may select those candidates to be interviewed from the application pool, or the human resources office may select likely candidates to be interviewed. Most principals will involve other administrators and teachers from their building in the selection process. The perceived excellence of the candidate in a purely instructional sense is not always the top priority of the principal. He or she will be looking for candidates who will be able to control a class of students and who will be able to relate to students in a positive manner. The principal is also looking for someone who will be a good team player and will be amenable to supervision by the principal.

The principal may also be looking for someone who can meet the needs of the school outside the classroom setting, perhaps as a basketball coach or newspaper advisor. Sometimes these extraneous considerations are given greater weight than they should be given. It is fair to say that for most principals, the academic background of the applicant is a necessary but not sufficient criterion for selecting the candidate.

This description of the hiring process assumes, of course, that there is a pool of candidates for the principal to choose from. Unfortunately, this is not true in all too many cases. In some urban districts at the secondary school level, many faculty members are teaching outside their area of academic expertise. Most states only permit this in situations where academically qualified candidates are not available.

This problem is also common in sparsely settled rural areas. Finding qualified teachers of physics or calculus in such rural schools is a daunting challenge. Suburban school districts surrounding the larger cities typically have the greatest access to qualified teaching candidates. A pool of qualified candidates is easier to attract at the elementary level, even in rural areas, because the certification requirements are broader, and elementary-certified teachers are more widely distributed across the general population.

The workaday world of the school principal is fast-paced, if not frenetic. A school principal often looks back on the day with few clear memories of what transpired. A typical day is a whirl of interactions with teachers, parents, and students, usually with the aim of solving specific management or interpersonal issues. A high school principal, for example, typically arrives at work by 7:00 a.m. and usually leaves for home at about 4:30 p.m. or later.

The hours in between are always interesting and challenging, but leave little opportunity for reflection or strategic thinking. In a school of 1,700 students in grades 9–12, there are usually three assistant principals to help with operating the school. Most principals try to carve out twenty minutes or so for a quick lunch in the faculty lunchroom. This interlude provides them with an opportunity to discuss school issues with classroom teachers in an informal setting.

The concrete reality of running a large organization on a daily basis molds most principals into managers who are very pragmatic, with little patience for theory and speculation. This attitude of the worker in the trenches often causes conflict with district office administrators who have the leisure of taking a more theoretical approach to the challenges of public education.

The basic reality is that whatever initiatives are developed by state or local officials need to be implemented at the building level. As in any human organization, there is a built-in resistance to edicts from above. Thus a principal must often convince skeptical teachers to enthusiastically implement new programs or procedures initiated with little or no input from the teachers or principals involved.

A principal is primarily judged on whether or not he or she "runs a tight ship." Preserving an orderly educational environment is clearly the task of the principal. It implies that he can both create an environment in which students cooperate with school rules and where the energies of the small number of truly disruptive students can be contained, if not redirected. This healthy school climate demands that the principal can induce his or her teachers to do the little things that promote a well-run school and a well-disciplined student body. These small routines include such basics as teachers taking attendance in each class, standing at their door between class periods to supervise students passing in the halls, and maintaining a productive learning environment within their own classroom.

The most typical student discipline breaches encountered in secondary schools involve students cutting class, altercations or fights among students, and serious misbehavior within the classroom. At an elementary level, typical discipline issues involve teasing other students, bus behavior problems, and students misbehaving within the classroom. These issues are minor on an individual basis but can undermine school climate if they are not dealt with quickly and consistently. Unfortunately, there are too many schools in this country where the number of even minor infractions simply overwhelm the resources of the school.

In the small number of schools where there are many serious disciplinary problems, minor issues are often ignored. This simply exacerbates the discipline problems in such schools, often leading to a downward spiral that makes these schools dysfunctional. This type of environment is dispiriting both to the teachers and administrators in the school. If good order cannot be maintained in a school, the students cannot succeed. Many principals in this type of environment begin to bunker down in their office, further contributing to a sense of drift, if not chaos, in the school.

To be truly effective, a school principal needs to be a "walks-the-halls" administrator. Such principals walk around their school in the morning as students and teachers arrive. These strolls through the school make it easy for teachers to stop the principal to talk about minor issues or concerns that can often be resolved before they become larger. This approach can be thought of as preventive maintenance for the organization. This type of principal also makes a quick walk around the school several other times during the school day.

Furthermore, teachers feel more comfortable talking with their principal on their own classroom turf rather than making a special trip to the school office. This visibility also makes the principal seem more approachable to students. As students interact with the principal they sometimes alert him or her to potential problems in the school or within an individual classroom. A principal of the "walk-the-halls" variety is constantly involved in a reconnaissance mission.

Parent meetings for the principal usually involve the resolution of some thorny issue. Perhaps a teacher and parent are having contentious disagreements about a student's performance or behavior. Or perhaps a student has become a serious discipline problem on a schoolwide basis. The principal, as well as the assistant principal, also become involved in parent meetings involving weapons charges, drug possession, or other criminal offenses.

Most of these meetings are disagreeable for all concerned, and principals seldom endear themselves to the parent in such confrontational situations. Over time a principal's friends come and go, but enemies accumulate. Disgruntled parents can do serious damage to a principal's reputation in the community over a period of time. To be successful as a principal, a person needs highly developed interpersonal and political skills based on solid integrity. An ability to discount unwarranted or petty criticisms is also a valuable asset for a principal.

An average high school principal spends about forty-five to fifty hours per week at school during the workday. After the students leave, he or she has time to meet with individual teachers or groups of teachers, usually in a departmental setting. She or he often wants to take a walk to the athletic fields to watch practice or attend games and matches. This provides a chance to interact with parents of student athletes on an informal basis.

Such conversations provide yet another finger on the pulse of the school. The high school principal spends another night or two per week attending school functions. These are as varied as back-to-school nights, athletic events, parent-teacher meetings, musical and dramatic productions, school board meetings, and other community meetings. Altogether, a typical high school principal works fifty-five to sixty hours per week during the school year. An elementary principal, with fewer night meetings, works about fifty hours per week during the school year.

Thus far, we have not discussed the supervision of teachers and the instructional program as a part of the principal's work life. For most principals, due to the pressures of daily management issues, teacher supervision and curriculum monitoring are given scant attention. Perhaps about 20 percent of elementary principals and 10 percent of secondary school principals give the instructional program the attention that it deserves. In larger districts, even in poorer urban areas, the district provides some curriculum and instruction specialists to monitor classroom instruction.

Remember that principals are not typically selected primarily for their instructional or curriculum expertise. While many principals can't find the time to attend to this question, there are actually many principals who really don't have great interest in instructional issues or who feel uncomfortable in addressing them. It's not that they don't consider the actual educational process important, but rather that they assume that these issues are being properly addressed by classroom teachers. In many larger or more affluent districts, there are a small cadre of instructional specialists who do assist teachers with purely instructional issues.

Given the ratio of teachers to building-level administrators, usually about 20 to 1, school principals tend to concentrate only on the small minority of teachers who are seriously deficient. These are the teachers who cannot control their classroom and who generate many complaints from both students and parents. A rule of thumb in management circles is that a first-level supervisor can properly monitor from five to eight immediate subordinates. School administrators have a far greater supervisory load while at the same time being responsible for the activities of hundreds, if not thousands, of students.

The principal should not ignore these problems with staff members, but, in those districts with militant teachers unions, they are very difficult to resolve. A principal who tries to remediate such teachers finds serious roadblocks in the teacher contract and with union officials who typically defend the teacher at every step in what is called the "progressive discipline" process.

Most union contracts as well as state laws and court decisions require that a progressive discipline process be followed before a teacher can be dismissed for incompetence. The first step in this process may be a verbal warning that a certain action, or inaction, should be addressed by the teacher. The next step is a written memo to the teacher outlining the concern and recommending remedial action. Teachers usually have a right to be represented by their union representative whenever they have a conference with a principal that might be construed as being in the nature of a reprimand.

If the problem is unresolved by this point, the principal must provide more formal written documentation of the issue. These documents are often referenced at a later date by union representatives to criticize the actions or approach of the principal. The next step is for the principal to provide the underperforming teacher specific recommendations for improvement.

In the state of Pennsylvania, as in many other states, the next step is for the teacher to be formally rated as unsatisfactory on the official state teacher evaluation form. In Pennsylvania, court and arbitration rulings have mandated that two consecutive unsatisfactory ratings are necessary to support a move for dismissal for instructional incompetence. Additionally, there must also be at least a few months between the two unsatisfactory ratings to give the teacher time to improve performance. The only exceptions to this cumbersome process are for cases of especially egregious actions by the teacher such as blatant disregard of students' safety or welfare, causing physical harm to the student, or illicit sexual activity involving students.

The teacher and his union have several choices about the venue for the dismissal hearing. One option is to have a hearing before the school board. Many decades ago a junior high principal was involved in a school board dismissal hearing for one of his teachers. The teachers union lawyer grilled the principal on the witness stand from 7:30 p.m. until 11:00 p.m. The union lawyer then questioned the teacher for less than half an hour. The school board ultimately dismissed the teacher, and the union appealed to the state department of education. The rationale for the appeal was that the hearing was unfair to the teacher because she did not take the stand until very late at night!

More recently a superintendent participated in a meeting about a poorly performing teacher at the point of the first unsatisfactory rating. This was the first experience for a new principal in a highly adversarial meeting of this kind. The teachers union brought in their regional representative, a man who frequently represents teachers at similar meetings. The union representative kept the principal on the defensive for the entire meeting. The meeting dealt more with the alleged shortcomings of the principal rather than the deficiencies of the teacher. It should not be surprising that principals are extremely reluctant to submit themselves to this type of interrogation by a hostile union representative. It is too simplistic to assume that weaker teachers unions or weaker tenure laws would expedite the cumbersome and complex process just described. Many existing legal requirements are embedded in state laws or court or arbitration rulings rather than in teachers' contracts or tenure laws.

Day-to-day relationships between the union and the school principal are generally fairly collaborative. Unless the principal is a martinet, the teachers in his or her school want to cooperate both on an interpersonal basis and for the good of the school. A principal's concerns with a teacher are sometimes mediated by the school's union representative or by other teachers who work closely with the teacher. This indirect and muted approach to resolving problems with teachers works well in many situations. Over time a good principal establishes a reputation for being firm but fair that will help resolve successfully instructional problems with teachers.

A common failing among building principals is that they tend to be too building-centric in their educational views. They naturally think in terms of the education of students in their particular school. A middle school principal, for example, thinks primarily of students in grades 6–8. Superintendents often have conversations with principals trying to give them the perspective of the student, who goes through the school district from grades K–12. A good principal considers the district as a whole and views the educational program in his or her school in the context of the entire district.

This chapter demonstrates the difficulty of the task faced by a school principal. A reader might wonder why someone would aspire to such a position. Most school principals derive great satisfaction from their work. It is very gratifying to work with individual students and see them achieve academically and thrive as human beings.

The same is true for the positive influence that a good principal can have on his or her staff. These positive impacts on teachers will occur in both the professional and personal dimensions. An effective principal also experiences satisfaction from competently leading a complex and essential public institution. Such principals earn the respect of their teachers, parents, and the general public. There are always a fair number of visionary and highly competent principals who lead schools that are excellent in every way. This job, with all of its challenges, is often very rewarding for those who choose it.

15

Special Education and Other Special Services

Until the 1960s our society's attitude toward the disabled was unworthy of a nation that views itself as compassionate. Students with even moderate physical and mental handicaps were kept out of the schools. These children languished in their homes with no attention to their serious problems. They were a heavy burden and worry to their parents. Regular public schools only educated the most moderately mentally challenged students. Most schools had one classroom with ten to fifteen of these students in a self-contained setting.

A visit to an upper-middle-class suburban junior high school in 1965 is instructive on the attitudes at the time. This school had a ninth-grade student who suffered from the delusion that he was an infantryman fighting the Nazis in World War II. After viewing too many movies he imagined that he was on the front lines tossing a hand grenade into the enemy lines.

He would run down the hall of the school, toss an imaginary grenade over his shoulder, and drop to the floor in a fetal position. The troubled boy then imitated the sound of the grenade exploding and would remain on the floor in this position for a minute or two. Finally, he would then get up and walk down the hall as if nothing had happened.

The teachers and students pretty much ignored these antics as an eccentric behavior by an otherwise quiet student. This boy needed help, but the schools at the time did not provide it. It is difficult to imagine such a student behaving this way in today's schools without quick intervention.

Any discussion of the impact of special education practices over the past forty years should be considered compassionately. Parents of most students are protective and defensive regarding the education of their children. This is doubly true for the parents of special needs children. The future of their special needs children causes constant anxiety and concern to these parents, making them more likely to view any discussion of the cost and complexity of special education as an attack on programs vital to their children.

A discussion of the rapidly rising cost of special services and their related impact on general education is not to imply that such services are not justifiable, but merely to acknowledge that such accommodations are extremely costly. While the many positive changes in the education of special needs children over the decades are a tribute to the sensitivity and creativity of our public educators, they are nonetheless extremely costly.

The Education of All Handicapped Act of 1975 accorded all mentally and physically handicapped students the right to a free and appropriate public education. Parents are now given the opportunity to participate in the development of an appropriate education for their students through the mandate that each student be given an Individualized Educational Program (IEP). This document requires the approval of the parent before it can be implemented. If the parent disagrees with the proposed program, and the school won't modify the program to the parent's satisfaction, the parent has a right to appeal the proposed program.

The concept of the "least restrictive environment" became prominent by the mid-1970s. The mandate required that each student be educated in an environment as close to that of a regular student as feasible. This concept fairly quickly led to the transfer of most disabled students from special schools back to their regular public schools. This dispersion of the special education population was undoubtedly a boon to the students and parents involved. Society, through its schools, was asserting the ethically sound principle that disabled students should participate in the mainstream of American life to the greatest extent possible.

At the same time, the incorporation of special education students into the regular school environment proved to be a great challenge to both teachers and administrators. Even such a seemingly simple issue as availability of suitable school facilities became a major issue in most school districts.

The new and smaller classes of special education students typically were housed in whatever classroom space could be found in the school. Before long there were demands from special education advocates to ensure that special education students in each school had facilities comparable to those of regular education students.

The least-restrictive-environment thrust also meant that special education students in each school could not be segregated from the regular school population more than absolutely necessary to remediate their educational deficits. This initiative gave rise to student designation as part-time or resource room special education students, depending upon the amount of time the student spends with a certified special education teacher. Students assigned to these programs typically leave their regular classes for one to three hours a day for targeted instruction in the basic skills subjects.

These part-time classes and resource rooms require additional staffing beyond the standard one classroom teacher for every twenty-five students. The involvement of both regular and special education teachers in the educational program of these students requires greater levels of communication among teachers, a necessity that requires both additional time and energy on the part of the regular classroom teacher.

A greater number of special needs students in regular classrooms also complicate the work of the teacher. Student IEPs often incorporate expectations and goals for students within the regular classroom. Some special needs students with social or emotional deficits exhibit poor impulse control. Such students are prone to acting-out behavior that can be a distraction for both the teacher and the other students from concentrating on academic instruction. In extreme cases the disruptive behaviors from these students can cause great anxiety or even fear on the part of the other students in the class.

IEPs began to require specific learning outcomes that the school committed to achieve with the students. As time passed, some parents of special needs students came to expect the same level of guarantees by the school for the achievement of regular education siblings of special education students. The onus on student achievement slowly shifted over time from the parents and students to the teachers and school.

Forty years ago the achievement of students was considered to be primarily a function of student effort and parent support. This attitude first shifted among special education parents so that the school was considered responsible for the achievement of its students, rather than the student himself or herself. By the 1990s the general conventional wisdom evolved to the belief that the school, rather than the student, was primarily responsible for student achievement.

This dramatic change in parent and student attitudes over the past forty years is not apparent to present-day parents and teachers. Parents in those days were reluctant to question the teacher's competence or goodwill. Nowadays many parents are quick to place the blame for poor student performance on the school or teacher rather than on the student.

This attitude is partially encouraged by the underlying assumption of special education law that poor student performance is a result of poor teaching or inappropriate instruction. The schools or the teachers are obviously the problem in some cases. More often, however, the lack of student achievement must be considered in the context of the student and her or his world.

The everyday experiences of students in their home and community greatly influence student performance.

An important aspect of special education services is that they often supplant rather than supplement regular instruction. Special education students are not given additional instructional time but rather are provided more appropriate instruction by specially trained teachers, usually individually or in small groups. Schools normally try to pull students from nonacademic portions of their regular curriculum rather than from core academic subjects. The complexities of scheduling a large number of special education students efficiently, however, sometimes requires that these students miss regular instruction in math, reading, or other basic subjects.

Students with disabilities that cause them to regress academically over the summer months are eligible to attend extended school year programs, at public expense, for six weeks or so during the summer. Federal law also makes children with certain disabilities eligible for publicly funded programs beginning at age three. These two relatively recent expansions to special education services have added billions of dollars to special education costs each year on a national basis.

The most important driver of special education expenses is the fact that classes are much smaller than in regular education. Furthermore, additional teachers are needed to operate pullout instruction to supplement regular classroom instruction. Consider an elementary school with twenty regular classroom teachers. Four additional teachers may be required to operate resource rooms and part-time special education classes.

Assuming an elementary school of five hundred students with twenty regular teachers, there will be about fifty special education students requiring pullout instruction by certified special education teachers. If the total compensation for each special education teacher averages $70,000, four teachers will cost $280,000. The additional cost to provided specialized instruction to these fifty students will approach $6,000 each year for each special education student. This is in addition to the average regular education cost per student of perhaps $12,000 a year or more.

Special education pullout programs also require extra classrooms. A new classroom costs about $250,000 to build. Four classrooms for the elementary school discussed previously would cost $1,000,000. This cost is usually amortized over twenty to thirty years in a bond issue at a yearly cost of perhaps $70,000. These additional rooms need to be cleaned every night by a custodian for perhaps another $10,000 per year.

In many school districts the addition of special education teachers implies an increase in supervisory personnel, usually at the district level. This is necessary because these teachers must prepare and implement an IEP for each student that will pass legal muster. Poorly crafted and poorly executed IEPs can be extremely costly to the district as well as harmful to the student.

Parents can challenge an IEP either at the development stage or can later argue that the teacher did not properly implement the IEP. Such a challenge can be appealed to the point where a special education hearing can be demanded. This hearing frequently requires the district to hire counsel and present a case before a hearing officer appointed by the state. These hearings can cost as much as $30,000 apiece.

Parents can also sue the district in the courts, which could result in significantly higher legal costs. Legal precedents from such proceedings can cascade into additional costs of millions of dollars statewide and perhaps hundreds of millions of dollars on a national basis. Thus the IEPs and the performance of the special education teachers need to be monitored much more closely than the performance of a regular education teacher.

Districts often employ such a special education supervisor for every twenty teachers or so at a cost of perhaps $100,000 per supervisor. Thus the four teachers in our hypothetical elementary school will generate an additional $20,000 per year in supervisory costs (assuming that one-fifth of the supervisor's time cost can be assigned to these four teachers).

Thus the total cost to an elementary school for these four teachers is $280,000 in teacher compensation, $20,000 in extra supervisory costs, $70,000 to provide the classrooms, and $10,000 to clean the classrooms—a total of $380,000 each year to provide these extra services to fifty students. This increases the cost above the regular instruction cost to more than $7,500 per special education student.

A major driver of increased special education expense in the past two decades has been the advent of what is known as the one-on-one aide. These support personnel are hired to accompany a single student throughout the school day. These aides are assigned to students with such severe mental or physical disabilities that they cannot function in a regular school environment without this full-time aide.

In previous decades these students would have attended special schools, often operated on a county basis, where they would have the assistance they need within a self-contained classroom. These classrooms often had a teacher with perhaps two or three aides for ten students. This was extremely costly, but not nearly as costly as current practice.

A single aide of this type could cost a school district more than $30,000 each year for salary and benefits. This raises the cost per student by $30,000 in addition to the cost for regular instruction. The demand by parents for this type of service is expanding rapidly. A recent staffing study for a Pennsylvania school district of twelve thousand students found that there were more than thirty such one-on-one aides in the district. Thus the district incurred a cost of about $1 million a year for these support personnel.

In this particular district there were a large number of non–English speaking immigrant students in certain parts of the district. In a second-grade classroom of twenty-eight students, most of the children could not speak English. The room also had six identified special education students as well as one seriously disabled student with a one-on-one aide. Is it any wonder that the significant number of students with special needs in this one class negatively affects the academic performance of these students? Should we be surprised that many teachers in such a frustrating situation leave teaching after a few years?

The discussion of the English-language learners (ELLs) in the previous paragraph points to another special program that became common in the schools about thirty years ago and that has grown geometrically over the past three decades. One reason for the outsize growth of this program is obviously the great increase in non–English speaking students that have entered our schools over the past few decades.

Forty years ago there were about three million Hispanic or Latino students in the public schools. Today there are more than ten million students of Hispanic background. About one-half of these students require ELL services of various types. The growth in these numbers explains why such programs have exploded in recent decades (Planty et al., 2009, 136). Since 1990, for example, the federal budget for these programs has ballooned from $200 million to $800 million a year. This represents only a small portion of total monies spent on ELL programs. The extra staffing required in local school districts to provide ELL services to these five million students requires annual expenditures of multiple billions of dollars on a national basis.

Many ELL programs operate in a similar manner to the special education programs described previously. Some students are pulled from their regular classes to meet with ELL teachers to provide the students with support to achieve in their regular classes. Students with little or no English fluency are placed in separate classes where instruction is provided in their native language. The other factor responsible for the large growth in this program is that students are quickly placed in such programs but slow to exit from them. This is a normal characteristic of bureaucratic behavior that is often self-protective and self-perpetuating.

The first large-scale federally funded remediation program is known as Title I. This program is designed to remediate poverty-level students who are performing poorly in reading or math. Congress passed this program in the mid-1960s. The program operates as a supplement to regular instruction, with students typically being taken from their regular classes for one-on-one or small-group instruction, usually by a teacher aide in a carefully structured program. The federal budget for this program has grown from $2.7 billion in 1980 to more than $14 billion in 2009. Most school districts rely solely on these federal pass-through funds to finance their Title I programs.

One recent experience by a superintendent involved a student with a peanut allergy. The incident offers a good example of how a request for a special service can significantly impact school costs. While not strictly speaking a special education issue, the request for costly special consideration is similar to the scenario that ensues in all requests for new special services.

Students with peanut allergies can go into anaphylactic shock when exposed to even minute particles of peanuts or peanut products. This reaction can affect several parts of the body and may be fatal. It is only reasonable that parents of these children would have real concerns about the safety of their children. In elementary schools, such students often are assigned to special lunch tables so that they are not exposed to peanut products that other students may bring to lunch, anything from peanut butter sandwiches to Snickers bars.

There is a medical device known as an EpiPen that students can use when needed to deliver medication to their body when they begin to have an allergic reaction. These devices can be used effectively by students who are about eight years of age or older. The situation at hand involved a six-year-old child whose mother insisted that a full-time aide be employed to accompany her child on the school bus to and from school each day. Acceding to this request would have cost at least $10,000 a year.

One solution might be for the bus driver to administer the EpiPen in an emergency. The private bus contractor, however, refused to permit this option. Once inside the school, a school nurse was always available to come to the classroom and administer the medication. Nevertheless, the teachers union became involved in the issue and released a memo to teachers stating that under no circumstances should they administer the EpiPen.

The principal took great pains, including practice sessions, to ensure that someone from the office would rush to the student in the classroom if for some reason the nurse were not available. Knowing that there were at least ten other cases of such allergies in the seven elementary schools, the superintendent could see that this request for an aide on the school bus would actually cost at least $100,000 per year to implement.

The district declined to provide the service once it realized that an eight-year-old sibling rode the bus with the six-year-old and knew how to administer the EpiPen. In this instance, the major additional costs were avoided. Yet the incident serves as a good example of how school costs can spiral upward even with issues having no relationship to the educational mission of the schools.

Public school critics who complain about the high costs of public schools have no understanding of the financial and professional burdens that public schools assume to provide this important social good. Charter, private, and parochial schools often accept only special needs students with milder disabilities. The burden of dealing with the most challenging and expensive cases rests with the public schools.

The attention and care provided by public school teachers to children in most need of extra attention and effort are a tribute to the millions of educators who work with these young people each day. The lessons that these educators indirectly teach to all students about compassion and caring for others are truly profound.

In ending this chapter, it is well to recall the earlier caution. To describe the extremely high cost of these programs is not to criticize or devalue them. There is no question that literally tens of millions of students have been significantly assisted by such programs over the last forty years. Most of these former students are now productively employed and leading fuller lives than would otherwise have been the case. This positive outcome not only adds to the general welfare of our society but also contributes to national productivity and wealth.

16

School Finance

In previous chapters we have touched upon the limitations on school boards in terms of raising revenue. We will now review the narrow limits in which a superintendent, school principal, or teacher can control the expenditure side of the budget. The political realities of school district operation practically force a superintendent to construct what is known as an *incremental budget*. All existing programs and expense items are assumed to go forward with an incremental increase.

It is always difficult to remove a program from the school budget because each line item in a budget has its own constituency, both internally and in the wider community. The constituency that fears a cut to its area will use whatever political pressure is available to maintain if not expand its budget. Because total revenues are constrained by the political process, it is difficult for a district to find new money to fund initiatives that might improve the instructional program.

The overriding constraints in school budget construction are class size and the number of teaching positions. There is a virtually universal agreement among teachers and parents that smaller class sizes, or at least maintaining current class sizes, are an imperative in every budget. Because staffing costs typically account for more than 70 percent of a school budget, locking class size at a certain level leaves little room for major initiatives.

If a superintendent were to recommend a 25 percent increase in class size, say from an average of twenty to twenty-five students in elementary school, the reaction from the teachers and the parents would be swift and raucous. Such an increase in average class size, however, would permit several policy options not affordable in a simple incremental budget.

The district, for example, could maintain its current cadre of teachers and significantly reduce the teaching load of each teacher, allowing much more time for lesson planning, training programs, and curriculum development. Or the money made available by larger class sizes could be used to increase teacher salaries. The extra monies could also be rechanneled into more teacher support positions or to fund significant increases in textbooks and instructional materials. Without debating the relative merits of these options, they do demonstrate that dramatic changes in school operations would be possible at present financing levels, if the class size issue could be addressed on a cost-benefits basis.

There are relatively few dramatic changes that can be made to the other 30 percent of the budget consumed by areas such as energy, transportation, building maintenance, and debt service. Without creating a major political controversy, a school board and superintendent can actually influence only a small percentage of the budget.

The budgeting situation at the building level is even more constrained. Principals often have limited input as to the number and types of personnel that will be assigned to their building. In many cases, principals have little control over the hiring decisions or the staff members assigned to their school. Many principals do have control over what is called the *instructional budget*. This mainly concerns textbook and supply budgets to operate the various programs in the school. Much of the supply budget is predetermined as the quantity of copy paper, art supplies, office supplies, and textbooks are fairly well constrained by the nature of the particular instructional budget.

There is some give-and-take in the building budget among departments and grade levels, depending on the extent to which they are able to influence the thinking of their principal. Often the freedom of the principal to allocate her instructional budget is influenced by district initiatives that imply the purchase of certain textbook series or the purchase of instructional equipment such as computers or other technology.

The level of control of a classroom teacher over the school budget is virtually nonexistent. Other than the aforementioned influence that can be exerted upon a principal at the department or grade level, teachers are expected to work with whatever they are given. Some school districts make mini-grants available to a few of their teachers to initiate programs or approaches that the teachers believe will improve instruction. Such programs are few and far between, however, and are not usually resourced well enough to make a significant difference.

Federal and state grants offer an option for a teacher, school, or district to secure financial resources that they would not otherwise have. The problem with such grants is that they tend to be targeted—limited to initiatives dictated by the state or federal government. These may or may not be suitable to the situation in a given school or district. Grants are also subject to the vagaries of the political process. Each new governor or president comes into office with his own policy ideas that are then supported by grant money. This reality accounts for the "this too shall pass" attitude of some veteran staff members.

Unfortunately, the initiatives of the previous administration are almost always cast aside, strangling new initiatives before they have time to mature and reach a scale that can be adopted by other school systems. This same dynamic is at work with grant monies made available to university professors who wish to conduct educational research projects. There have been many programs over the years that have had real potential to improve instruction, but are eventually starved for funds and then discontinued.

Following the money in education leads inevitably to state policies on school funding. Almost a century ago states began looking at how they could collect and then distribute funds for schools in a manner that would provide a basic education to all children. The plans developed were generally known as *foundation programs.*

The idea was that regardless of the wealth of a given school district, enough state money would be provided to ensure at least a basic level of education to all students. Most states eventually passed legislation that, if implemented, would have allowed poorer school districts to properly educate their students.

The problem has always been the tendency of state legislatures to underfund the formulas that they create. In Pennsylvania the now-abandoned formula called for the state to contribute an average of 50 percent of the instructional costs for school districts. As recently as the 1970s, state funding for basic education approached this 50 percent goal. In recent years, however, the Pennsylvania basic instructional subsidy supports only about 35 percent of instructional costs. The percentage of instructional costs covered by the state has been declining slowly over the years. This dynamic has also occurred in many other states.

State foundation formulas are structured so that per-pupil allocations for the poorer school district are much larger than allocations for more affluent districts. Some districts may receive 75 percent of their total budget from the state while the wealthiest districts may receive less than 10 percent of their funding from the state.

The nature of these state subsidies is such that legislators from wealthier school districts have little incentive to increase funding for the basic subsidy. Also, since the major sources of income for the state are income taxes and sales taxes, wealthier communities pay a larger percentage of any tax increases that may be enacted to support greater subsidies.

Legislators from less affluent districts have an incentive to increase subsidies because districts that they represent will receive more funding while they will pay a disproportionately smaller amount of any required tax increases. These conflicting interests create a great deal of controversy in state legislatures each year at budget time. The level of state funding for schools in most states will wax and wane depending on the mix of political interests currently dominating the state legislature.

The national economy also plays a large role in the level of funding in the basic subsidy. When the economy is booming, state income tax and sales tax revenues increase and school funding becomes more generous. In a bad economy, as we've seen for several years now, state revenues plateau or even decrease. This causes declines in available funding for schools. This dynamic played out in Hawaii in 2009 to the point where the school year for students was cut from 180 days to 163 days.

This cutback in the school year is virtually unique in recent times. The money saved by the state was a function of the state teachers union agreeing to seventeen days of furloughs for their members. As the 2010 school year approached, a growing number of school districts were considering a four-day week in an attempt to reduce the school budget.

When state funding is cut or frozen, the poorer districts are disproportionately affected. Since a larger part of the total budget comes from the state in less affluent districts, a cut in state funds blows a large hole in the budget. Since such state cuts are usually a reflection of a bad economy, the less affluent districts cannot easily increase local property taxes in such an economic environment. Wealthier districts, however, are not as negatively affected because a comparatively small part of their total budget is dependent on state funding. Bad economic conditions are causing our society to regress in terms of providing equal educational opportunities for our most vulnerable students.

While per-pupil expenditures in high-poverty urban districts are much less than many affluent suburbs surrounding our big cities, they do rank around the middle of school expenditures on a national basis. This fact obscures the reality that the peripheral costs of operating in a disadvantaged urban environment are much greater than in suburban or rural school districts, leaving much less money available for the core educational mission of the schools.

The most obvious peripheral cost in urban schools is school security. Schools in disadvantaged urban neighborhoods find that the violent crimes against persons and property in the neighborhood spill over into the schools. Schools in such neighborhoods need a cadre of security guards, as well as security cameras and the staff to monitor them. Such precautions are generally very minimal in suburban and rural areas.

The parental and community support for these urban schools is much lower than in other schools. There is a high school in Philadelphia, for example, that finds it necessary to call the homes of its students every morning at 6:30 a.m. to encourage parents to send their child to school. A lack of coping skills among some parents requires a higher number of ancillary personnel to help these parents deal with basic child-rearing activities.

The administration of the Philadelphia school district has also notified building principals that the percentage of students participating in the free breakfast program will be one metric used in the evaluation of the principal. Two generations ago, it was assumed that parents would provide breakfast for their children. A generation ago free breakfasts were made available in low-income areas so that students did not need to rely on parents to provide them with breakfast. We have now reached the point where many parents aren't sufficiently motivated to send their children to school early enough to participate in the free breakfast program.

Schools in disadvantaged urban settings need to employ home and school visitors and social workers to actively interact with the students and parents on the home front. These categories of personnel are far less common in sub-urban and rural school districts. High schools in many inner cities experience daily student absentee rates of 25 percent or higher. Such an absentee rate means that the average student misses one out of four school days.

Given a 180-day school year, the average student in such a school misses 45 days of classes in a typical year. Students with this tentative attachment to the educational mission of the school cannot be expected to be active participants in the educational program on the days that they do attend. Is it any wonder that average student achievement in such an environment is so poor?

Special education programs are extremely costly due mainly to the high staffing levels necessary to support students properly in these programs. In many disadvantaged urban schools over 20 percent of students are assigned to such programs. This compares to about 13 percent of students in special education programs in the majority of school districts.

Some critics of special education maintain that schools try to have students identified as special education so as to secure more state and federal funding. This is not the case. The share of special education funding borne by the lo-cal districts keeps increasing so that there is not a financial advantage at the local level for a larger special education population, and there is usually a large financial disincentive.

The special problems unique to poor urban districts, as discussed previously, easily account for 25 percent of total expenditures in these schools. Not only can these expenses not be reduced but they must also be increased significantly before they can fully counteract the overwhelming disadvantages that schools and students in such neighborhoods face.

One method to compare school expenditures over time is as a percent of gross domestic product (GDP). In 1965 elementary and secondary school expenditures amounted to 3.9 percent of GDP. By 2007 this measure had increased to 4.6 percent of GDP (Planty et al., 2008, 45). By this measure, our country is allocating a slightly higher proportion of its wealth to public education than it did more than forty years ago.

There has been, however, a tremendous increase in expenditures on a dollar basis. Of course, we are a far wealthier country than we were forty-five years ago. The elements behind this great dollar increase are discussed later in this chapter. Although the dollar increase for staff salaries has grown dramatically, this is as much a function of greater numbers of staff members as of higher salaries for the average teacher or other employee.

Another perspective on school costs, mentioned with tongue firmly in cheek, is to consider schools purely as custodial institutions. Although schools teach most students how to read, write, and count, they also keep fifty million children off the streets for 180 days per year. Perhaps ten to fifteen million parents would not be able to participate in the workforce if it weren't for the fact that their children can be sent to school everyday at no direct cost to the parents. The productivity of these ten to fifteen million adults surely adds at least 10 percent to our nation's GDP. Thus investing less than 5 percent of GDP in the schools, purely from an economic viewpoint, seems like a very good return on investment.

Compare the cost of the custodial function of the schools to other means of paying for childcare. If the average per-pupil cost of schools nationally is about $12,000, this translates to an hourly cost of about $12 per hour. In many parts of the country, to hire a babysitter to watch your child while you treat yourself to dinner and a movie would cost about the same on an hourly basis, with little expectation that the children will learn something from the experience. Enrolling a young child in preschool costs about $50 per day. Sending your child to franchised tutoring centers such as Sylvan or Huntington costs $50 an hour or more.

Looking at school costs in this context reveals that they are fairly economical. Remember also that the cost of schooling typically includes round-trip bus transportation, the availability of a school nurse if the child becomes ill, and federally subsidized nutritious meals at lunchtime and often for breakfast. Schools are a reasonable investment even before we successfully teach most of our students to read and write well.

Turning our attention to dollar cost increases in education on a national level shows some truly startling statistics. In 1965 the amount spent on elementary and secondary education was $28 billion. By 2007 this number had soared to $631 billion (Planty et al., 2008, 45).

A portion of this dollar increase can be explained simply by general cost of living increases over this period. By 2007, $6.58 was required to purchase the same goods and services that cost $1.00 in 1965 (American Institute for Economic Research, n.d.). By this calculation, the services provided by schools in 1965 for $28 billion would have cost $184 billion in 2007. This is still a long way from $631 billion.

There are now fifty million public school students compared with forty-five million in 1965. This 10 percent increase in pupil population can account for an additional $18 billion cost increase for a total of $202 billion.

The paragraphs that follow provide an informed estimate of the increased costs over these forty-five years by major categories. The numbers generated are informed estimates designed to explain how school costs could have reasonably increased from $28 billion to over $600 billion over this time period.

The dollars required for staff salaries have increased dramatically. This is a reflection of both greater numbers of staff members as well as increased salaries for the average teacher and other school personnel. In 1970, there were 2.1 million public elementary and secondary teachers. By 2007 this number had increased to 3.2 million teachers (Planty et al., 2008, 18). If these 1.1 million new teachers on average earn $65,000 each in salary and related benefits, the cost for these extra teachers is $72 billion. This brings the total additional costs compared with 1965 to $274 billion.

This forty-five-year period saw a tremendous increase in the total number of school employees. In 1965 there were about 2.6 million school employees of all types. By 2006 there were approximately 6.2 million school employees (Snyder, Dillow, and Hoffman, 2009, 117). All comparisons in this discussion represent full-time-equivalent personnel. We first review these increases by major category and attempt to estimate the extra cost of these additional personnel in various staffing assignments. We explore why these staffing increases have occurred and why they may be both reasonable and necessary.

In 1965 there were about fifty-five thousand central office administrators and instructional coordinators. By 2006 this number had grown to 125,000. If we assume that the average salary- and payroll-related costs for each new administrator is $120,000, the total cost for these seventy thousand additional personnel is approximately $8 billion. At the building level the number of principals and assistant principals has increased from 75,000 in 1965 to 155,000 in 2006. Assuming that the salary and associated costs for these eighty thousand additional personnel averages $100,000 per administrator, the total cost for these additional personnel is $8 billion.

Schools have added a large number of guidance counselors, social workers, and school psychologists. The number of guidance counselors alone has increased from 30,000 in 1965 to 104,000 in 2006. If salary and related benefits for these extra seventy-four thousand counselors is $80,000, the total extra cost for these personnel is $6 billion. These categories of additional costs bring the total to $298 billion.

The extremely large increase in instructional aides and other support staff has contributed greatly to higher educational costs. In 1965 there were approximately fifty thousand instructional aides. By 2006 this number had grown to 705,000. If we assume that the average salary and related costs for these extra 655,000 aides is $30,000, the total new cost approaches $20 billion. The number of other support staff (secretaries, clerks, custodians, maintenance personnel, security guards) has increased from 500,000 in 1965 to 1,800,000 in 2006. Assuming salary and related costs at $40,000 for each of these support staff members, the total extra cost for these 1,300,000 extra personnel is approximately $52 billion. This brings our total expense to $370 billion.

School employee health insurance premiums represent another outsize contribution to the cost of public education. Health benefits for school employees are typically very generous compared with those provided to most Americans. For the purpose of this discussion, we assume that five million of the more than six million school employees are covered by health insurance by their school district. We further assume that the average cost per employee is $10,000 (assuming a mix of single and family coverage among employees). The cost of this benefit would approximate $50 billion ($10,000 × 5 million).

In 1965 there was not even a line item in school budgets to reflect technology purchases. By 1990 computers for both students and staff were ubiquitous in classrooms and offices. The staff required to maintain these computers and to instruct staff and students in their use are included in the previous paragraphs on staffing increases. A reasonable estimate is that hardware, software, and licensing agreement costs with computer and software vendors have added at least $5 billion annually to school costs.

The energy crisis of the 1970s also affected schools significantly in terms of utility and transportation costs. These greater-than-inflationary increases in transportation expenses raised the amount spent in this category to $20 billion. This occurred because today a greater percentage of students are transported to school than forty-five years ago and in some states school districts must transport private school students. Transportation costs increased from less than $1 billion in 1965 to approximately $20 billion in 2006, about $15 billion beyond inflationary increases. On a per-pupil basis, transportation costs have increased from $51 to $746 (Snyder et al., 2009, 251).

Utility costs for schools have increased significantly beyond inflationary increases. This is mostly a reflection of increases in the cost of oil and other fuels over this forty-five-year period. We can reasonably estimate that energy costs have increased by at least $5 billion beyond inflation over this period. These last two items have nothing to do with education and yet they contribute greatly to the increasing costs of operating our schools. Capital outlay and interest in debt account for an additional $72 billion (Snyder et al., 2009, 250). Our total costs identified at this point are $517 billion.

One common criticism of the skyrocketing cost of public education posits that increases in teacher salaries, necessitated by addressing the pressures of militant unions, is a major driver of increased costs. The data provided here does not address teacher salaries other than to assume that teacher salaries have increased at the rate of inflation. In 1965 the average teacher salary in the United States was $6,500. By 2007 the average had increased to $52,300 (Planty et al., 2008, 115).

To keep pace with inflation, this 2007 salary number would have been about $43,000 rather than $52,300. Thus the average salary for teachers increased by $9,300 or about 22 percent above inflation over this forty-two-year period. Adding this 22 percent to teachers' salaries raises the overall cost of education since 1965 by another $30 billion to about $547 billion, within striking distance of the actual number of approximately $631 billion in 2007.

The increase in teacher salaries above the inflation rate is certainly a positive development. Comparing increases in teacher salaries to wage increases across the economy over these four decades, however, reveals that teachers did not make noticeable progress relative to other workers. Teachers still earn somewhat more than the average salary for all American workers, but earn about 30 percent less than the average of twenty-three comparable professional occupations (DiCarlo, Johnson, and Cochran, 2008, 12).

Our economy today is much more productive than it was forty-five years ago and part of this increased productivity is reflected in rising wage rates across all occupations. In 1965 teachers on average earned just a little above the national average worker's salary. This same relationship still existed in 2007. For all of the rhetoric over the years that teachers in America should be better paid, the improvement has been modest at best.

A review of these data on increases in school costs by category over the years reveals that relatively little of the tremendous increase in costs can be attributed to teachers improving their financial lot relative to the rest of society. This is a major reason why it is just as difficult to recruit talented young people to teaching today as it was in the 1960s, or the 1920s for that matter.

The impact of legal expenses and requirements on school costs is impossible to calculate in a thorough manner. There is the direct cost of legal fees for lawyers and school district solicitors that have increased geometrically over the years. These costs surely total at least several billion dollars a year compared with minimal expenses forty-five years ago. By far, the larger costs are in the personnel required to implement court orders and legal precedents in special education and student disciplinary matters. These requirements play a significant role in the number of school personnel required and thus directly affect school costs.

While the Department of Education accounts for another significant increase in educational costs, most of these costs are pass-through funds to states and districts and are therefore already reflected in the previous discussion. The major pass-through expenses are for programs such as Title I and Special Education. President Carter created the Department of Education in the late 1970s. In the intervening thirty years, this department has evolved from a small startup organization to a behemoth with a budget of approximately $71 billion (Office of Management and Budget, 2010, 67–68). As recently as 1980, the budget for the Department of Education was $14 billion.

The tremendous dollar increase in education costs is largely a function of the growth in public education employment from 2.6 million in 1965 to 6.2 million in 2006. The 50 percent increase in the teaching corps can be explained by a 10 percent increase in enrollment, the large number of new special education positions over the decades, and the slow but steady move toward smaller class size.

How can we account for the explosive growth of employment in other personnel categories? The number of both district-level and building-level administrators has more than doubled. Administrative supervision tasks have increased dramatically given that there are 50 percent more teachers and double or triple the number of other professional and support personnel.

The enormous burdens to meet legal requirements relating to special education, the rights of employees to due process, and mandated student disciplinary procedures also imply a need for more administrative time and effort. Administrators must carefully document all actions involving special education students and carefully document disciplinary interactions with both staff members and students.

These obligations require more than simply completing paperwork. The administrator must be present at multiple meetings with parents and staff members and respond to legal challenges to proposed school actions. She must also be responsive to inquiries from parents and community groups on issues ranging from student suspension hearings to the menu for school lunches. Increasing demands for transparency and community involvement all require preparation and participation by school administrators.

The number of guidance counselors has increased more than threefold over the past forty-five years. This became necessary as the schools adopted a more therapeutic approach to student misbehavior and became more deeply involved in helping students to cope with troubled family situations. The increasing number of students with drug, alcohol, or psychological problems has also necessitated more counselors, psychologists, and social workers on the school payroll.

The number of instructional aides has increased largely due to special education requirements. Many more aides also have found their way into the regular classroom setting to assist teachers with large classes or to work with a few students who have weak impulse control. The more than tenfold increase in the number of instructional aides contributes a great deal toward the increasing cost of education. The growing number of instructional aides necessary to maintain computer labs and computer systems are typically assigned to this staffing category.

Support staff positions have increased from 500,000 to 1,800,000, mainly as a function of the increased paperwork requirements to operate a school district in a legally defensible fashion. Most school districts now employ a number of aides to carefully track attendance and to process disciplinary referrals in a legally defensible fashion. The exponential growth of security personnel in school districts is also reflected in the number of additional support staff positions.

In summary, the chief causes of the great increase in school costs include general inflation; a 10 percent increase in the number of students; new support services such as Title I, ELL programs, and an explosion of special education services; and outsize budget increases in the areas of health insurance, energy, transportation, and technology costs. Local school board members and superintendents have been hard-pressed over this entire period to find extra money to improve general education once the requirements for these categories were included in the budget each year.

Public school critics seldom dig down into the numbers to study the many reasons for the substantial increase in the costs of public schools over the decades. Too many critics prefer to assume that much of the increased expenses are the result of a bloated bureaucracy managing poorly. Other critics cite teachers unions as the primary scapegoat responsible for the dramatic increases in school costs.

This review demonstrates that the increases in school costs are a reaction to changes in the student body, greater parental and community expectations over the decades, and exogenous factors such as health insurance premiums and energy costs. Schools have generally met their obligation to respond to public demands while attempting to educate students effectively in a significantly more complex and challenging environment.

17

Schools as Organizations

An underlying theme of this book is an explanation of why school reform efforts over the past forty years have largely failed to gain traction. Thus far we have discussed many practical reasons for the lack of significant gains in student performance. In this chapter we explore some of the research-based findings from organizational theory that affect school performance. The pundits and politicians who champion various educational reforms not only fail to give sufficient attention to these organizational issues, but in too many cases they are unaware that such issues exist.

Repeated failed attempts at school reform at the federal, state, and local levels suggest that our standard approaches to school reform are fundamentally flawed. Substantive reform in a complex system such as a school district requires a level of organizational sophistication and unity of purpose that is seldom attainable under current school governance models.

Over the years there have been hundreds of successful school reform efforts at the school district and individual school levels. In virtually every case, however, these successful initiatives have failed to be adopted on a wide scale. This is because most school organizations fail to exemplify one or more of the five dimensions of schools as organizations that affect school performance. They are as follows: leadership theory, local politics and governance, state and national school politics, organizational theory, and change theory.

LEADERSHIP THEORY

Leadership theory deals with how leaders put themselves into position to make significant change in an organization. Peter Senge's work portrays an effective leader as both a reflective and highly moral individual (Senge, 1990). He describes a leader who has been in the position long enough to establish trust and to build a culture of teamwork.

Stephen Covey's views parallel Senge's insights concerning the need for a leader to reflect on his or her own personal beliefs and to develop the skills necessary to work for change collaboratively. Covey's notion of a "character ethic" is similar to Senge's emphasis on the personal character of the leader (Covey, 1991). A superintendent, by the nature of the position, has little time for the reflection that Covey believes is critical to good leadership. It is also difficult for a superintendent to work collaboratively with school boards with a frequent change in the cast of characters.

LOCAL POLITICS AND GOVERNANCE

Local politics and governance is yet another challenge. The politics of local school districts and the tendency toward micromanagement by many school boards can seriously inhibit a board's policy-making function and weaken a superintendent's ability to sustain reform. School boards that confuse their policy role with the administrative role that is rightly the domain of the superintendent and her or his staff are a major reason why superintendents leave a school district.

Indeed, some American school boards spend up to a quarter of their time dealing with problems of their own children or the issues involving children of relatives and close friends (Grady and Bryant, 1991, 68–72). Most superintendents find this problem to be relatively minor, but not insignificant.

The political imperatives of local school board governance militate against the development and implementation of long-range plans. The tenure of a typical board member in the United States is about seven years. Coupled with the adversarial nature of many board elections, this short tenure both erases institutional memory and undermines the consistency of mission necessary to achieve substantive reform. Successful school reform depends on the school board's ability to maintain a steady course despite changes in the superintendency and even changes in the membership of the board.

Visionary leadership by a board and superintendent presupposes sufficient time to develop a shared vision. Developing a cohesive team requires a level of trust and mutual respect that is one of the fruits of longer-term professional relationships. The time required to form such trusting relationships is simply not available to many school superintendents and boards. Indeed, the average tenure of superintendents is now only about four years. It is even shorter for many superintendents of large urban districts. While the average board member serves for seven years, there are still a few changes in school board membership during almost every election cycle.

The relatively short tenure of board members and superintendents is often a function of political controversies within a school community, often centering on funding and tax issues. A twenty-year review of property tax changes in fifty-five Pennsylvania school districts indicates that districts with the highest rates of increases in property taxes also had the highest level of board turnover. A high level of board member turnover leads in turn to higher levels of turnover at the superintendent level (McAdams, 1995, 57–70).

Power struggles between the superintendent and the school board, rather than mutual trust, often emerge from this constantly changing swirl of personalities. The political infighting that such struggles and clashes engender can be fatal to the sprit of collaboration and common purpose that is required to sustain school reform.

Superintendents are clearly vulnerable to political shifts on their school boards and become the victims of the often-whimsical priorities and enthusiasms of ever-changing boards. Superintendents must be nimble enough to change with the turnover in board priorities—or comfortable with frequent relocations. In either event, bold leadership over the long term is the exception rather than the rule.

STATE AND NATIONAL SCHOOL POLITICS

The vagaries of local political winds could be somewhat lessened if coherent education policy initiatives existed at the state or national levels. The interplay of governmental bodies, political parties, and special interest groups, however, has repeatedly stymied efforts at systemic educational reform. Conflicts among competing interests are exacerbated in large urban districts, where there is a greater diversity among constituencies. This is just one daunting challenge among many that afflicts leaders in our urban school districts that enroll 25 percent of our students.

John Chubb and Terry Moe have argued that the political nature of American public schools is a fatal impediment to significant school reform (Chubb and Moe, 1990). The heart of their argument is that conflict, rapidly changing priorities, a tendency toward micromanagement, and cumbersome controls are essential characteristics of the political process.

Chubb and Moe found that the most effective schools were characterized by a high level of professional autonomy at the individual building level, a condition that seldom exists in a highly politicized environment. Their solution at the time, the early 1990s, was to use privatization to achieve substantive school reform.

Their work, along with that of Milton Friedman, gave rise first to the school voucher movement and more recently to the charter school movement. Both of these initiatives have offered hundreds of thousands of students an alternative to failing schools, mostly in our large, urban districts. After twenty years, however, it cannot be claimed that vouchers or charter schools have had a wide-reaching impact on public education.

Seymour Sarason offered a similarly somber prognosis for public schools. After decades of studying school reform, he concluded that there is virtually no chance that reform will come from within the system. He believed that the stakeholders simply have too much to lose and warned that, if the governance issue were not faced, schools would get worse and public schools would ultimately be abandoned (Sarason, 1990).

Sarason's prediction has not come true, more likely because of the American attachment to public schools rather than due to any marked improvement in the schools. After decades of improvement efforts in individual schools, as well as state and federal initiatives, it appears that the schools thus far have proven impervious to sustained and widespread reform.

At the state level, the normal machinations of the political process have a major impact on education policy and practice. The terms of governors essentially bracket the time frame for change on educational issues. The dynamics of the political process dictate that each new governor will develop a plan for improving, if not radically reforming, public education.

The initiatives of the previous administration are always downplayed, and in many cases they are flatly repudiated. Meanwhile, battle-weary local school officials frequently adopt a "this too shall pass" attitude. If it can take four to five years for lasting positive change to be institutionalized at the local level, how much more constraining is the term of office of a governor in his or her attempts to reform education at the state level?

A study of six southeastern states—Alabama, Florida, Georgia, Mississippi, North Carolina, and South Carolina—demonstrates the difficulty of instituting educational reform at the state level (Southeast Regional Vision for Education, 1994). Only two of the top thirty-six education policy makers in these six states were still in office after ten years. The normal turnover in seats in the six state legislatures and in the governors' mansions during this ten-year period ensured that there would be little institutional memory regarding the successes and failures of educational reform.

This same study reported that on-again, off-again reform initiatives were a direct result of political instability and budget shortfalls. The authors concluded that the time necessary to initiate positive change in schools is longer than the tenure of political officials. Teachers in the trenches, they said, had grown "improvement weary."

The same undermining of school reform initiatives because of changes in political leaders also takes place at the national level. The No Child Left Behind law was passed in 2001 with much fanfare and bipartisan political support in Congress. Eight years later, a new administration of a different party is basically renouncing No Child Left Behind and is implementing a new federal initiative on school reform. Without addressing the strengths or weaknesses of the two initiatives, the point is simply that both state and national school improvement efforts rarely exist long enough for them to have the desired effect.

ORGANIZATIONAL THEORY

Leadership and political issues aside, significant organizational characteristics of schools also impede reform efforts. The major influence of the external environment on the operation of school districts makes the schools an excellent example of an "open system."

The local community powerfully influences education policy and practice. The community provides the students, while parents and the general public are greatly interested in taxes and property values—if not in high-quality education. In fact, many school staff members play a dual role as employees and parents or community members.

To be successful, a major school reform must enjoy a community consensus that extends well beyond the requirements for internal team building and shared vision in private organizations. Decision making by consensus slows down the change process and often dilutes the magnitude and effectiveness of the change attempted. American schools, by design, feature much more community involvement than do schools in other industrialized nations.

From an internal perspective, schools can be thought of as "loosely coupled systems." As such, each school can be considered a semiautonomous unit. Educational reformers such as Theodore Sizer, Robert Slavin, James Comer, and Henry Levin have labored for decades to improve schools on a one-by-one basis. Principals and teachers in a school are seldom willing to adopt reform models developed for other schools in their district or region.

Many of their ideas and strategies were excellent, and yet they could not be scaled up to positively affect schooling on a wide basis. This loosely coupled model may be the norm for schools. It is, however, a serious obstacle for those who would initiate statewide or even district-level reform.

Even if the resistance to top-down reform could be overcome at the building level, there would still be major resistance by individual teachers. Mintzberg defined five types of organizations, one of which is a "professional bureaucracy" (Bolman and Deal, 1991, 88). This organizational type is the norm in most schools, which feature a large core of classroom teachers who perform the critical activities of the organization.

Mintzberg's professional bureaucracy is characterized by autonomy at the operational level. The autonomy of the professional makes it very hard to make a systemic change from above. Teachers view themselves as professionals who use their professional judgment to make decisions about instructional goals and strategies. They also view themselves as interested and concerned about the welfare of their students and will resist strongly any changes that they believe will turn them into mere clerks or functionaries.

Teachers view principals and central office administrators as middle managers, who they believe should play a supportive and subordinate role in the actual instructional process. Teachers jealously guard their professional prerogatives to determine instructional methods within the classroom. Convincing a critical mass of teachers to adopt a major reform project, especially one directly affecting instruction, is a time-consuming process fraught with practical and political difficulties.

CHANGE THEORY

Michael Fullan carefully analyzed major school reform efforts over several decades and reached some compelling conclusions about the nature of the change process. Not surprisingly, he found that substantive change is both a time-consuming and an energy-intensive process. He concluded that "the total time frame from initiation to institutionalization is lengthy, [and] even moderately complex changes take from three to five years, while major restructuring efforts can take five to ten years" (Fullan, 1991, 49). Fullan continues to develop and refine these themes in his recent works *Leading in a Culture of Change* (2001) and *The New Meaning of Educational Change* (2007).

We have already seen how the short tenure of board members and superintendents and the influence of politics work against the institutionalization of school reform. A third phenomenon, which Fullan calls the *implementation dip*, further undermines reform efforts in public schools.

The implementation dip is the period early in the implementation process during which productivity and morale both decline. This is because of the tensions and anxieties generated as educators, parents, and students attempt to deal with unanticipated problems. Political demands for accountability and expectations for quick results often assert themselves at just this stage of the change process. Many promising reforms have been discarded prematurely during this period.

Thus far we have assumed that change is primarily a rational process. In reality, organizations change only when the people in them are willing and able to do so. In addition to strictly structural and political considerations, the prospective change agent must draw on motivational theories in planning for meaningful change.

Moving from the individual to the organizational level, we find that the assumptions, values and norms of the organization itself are powerful influences on the change process. All of these phenomena can be considered as constituting the culture of the organization. Just as the character of a person is deep-seated and resistant to change, the culture of an organization is also difficult to influence.

Indeed, many proposed changes are viewed as threats to the existing culture and are resisted for that reason alone. Phillip Schlechty, a nationally prominent advocate for school reform, affirms, "Structural change requires cultural change" (Schlechty, 1990, xvi). Thus one can say that a school needs to be "recultured" before it can be restructured.

Unfortunately, many would-be change agents, from school principals to governors to secretaries of education, seem unaware of the impact of school culture on the change process. The history of education reform is littered with reforms that failed or had adverse effects because those championing the effort had only the most superficial and distorted conception of the culture of the schools they sought to change.

The role of community and school culture in retarding or advancing positive change is pivotal. While there are always examples of superstar principals or superintendents who can significantly improve schools or districts, these are the exception rather than the rule.

For schools to improve significantly, it is necessary for the culture of the schools themselves to change. A healthier school culture would make it possible for administrators of even average ability to move their schools forward. The same dynamic operates at the teacher level. Even in the poorest schools there are stellar teachers who have a positive impact on students. As the culture of a given school improves, many heretofore-mediocre teachers become more effective.

The challenge is to develop a school environment or culture that is more conducive to helping teachers move from good to great. It is not reasonable to expect even potentially outstanding educators to thrive in schools with an impaired culture for learning.

Forty-plus years in dealing with parents and communities prompts several conclusions about America's general viewpoint toward education and schooling. Most parents have a generally positive attitude toward their schools. This is true both in very wealthy districts and in districts with extremely limited resources. There are few sustained critiques of school performance or a demand for higher performance from the parents or the community.

Shaw's aphorism that "democracy is that form of government that ensures that people are never governed better than they deserve" aptly describes the notion that people usually have the kind of schools that they want. This is to say that the average school community does not exhibit the same level of concern about school quality that is promulgated by think tanks and among the pundit class.

Most parents want their children to succeed in school and to be content with their teachers. They want their students to be sufficiently well educated to succeed in the economy. There are relatively few parents nationally, however, who push their children to high achievement. On balance, parents who do pressure or strongly urge their children toward high performance in fact have students who usually perform at a high level.

Where you have schools with a high level of parent support and encouragement for their students, you generally have schools that perform well. In educational parlance, these are schools that exhibit high "academic press." These schools tend to be more plentiful in more affluent districts given these are the areas that have more highly educated parents who place a higher value on education.

Such high performance–oriented schools and communities are not the norm on a national basis. These characteristics certainly don't exist in our large urban school districts. They are also scarce in semirural or rural areas of the country. Taken together, these districts with a more lackadaisical attitude toward school achievement represent more than 50 percent of all schools and students. At the risk of making an error in judgment, many parents simply do not have lofty academic aspirations for their children. They want their children to have a good occupation, eventually build a life with a spouse and family, and live at a convenient distance from Mom and Dad.

Critics of public schools often point to charter schools as the solution to improving our poorly performing public schools. They cite the fact that in some poorly performing districts, many more parents apply for charter schools than there are available slots to accommodate the applicants. Perhaps 10 percent of parents in a given attendance area of an undesirable school may apply to send their children to a charter school, but where are the other 90 percent of parents with children in these schools?

Public schools in areas where charter schools flourish are often demonstrably and obviously abysmal. Such parents either don't know or don't care that their children are being crippled for life by the disastrous state of their local schools. There is a deeply ingrained cultural attitude among many parents in these communities that school quality is not important. It is a tremendous trib-ute to the 10 percent of parents from these communities that who make Hercu-lean efforts to ensure that their children receive a high-quality education.

An example of a cultural circumstance that impedes achievement in Amer-ica's schools is the calendar for our school year. We have a deeply ingrained tradition of scheduling ten to twelve weeks of summer vacation for our stu-dents each year. Although originally a reflection of our agricultural past, the school calendar remains unchanged one hundred years after the majority of our citizens left the farms.

Today parents look forward to this summer period to schedule vacations and to enroll their students in special athletic or academic camps. It simply never occurs to most people that there might be a better way to schedule the school year. Other industrialized countries have a shorter summer vacation period but have several two-week holiday periods during the school year.

This practice in foreign countries provides more breaks from routine during the school year, but more importantly it prevents the regression in academic skills that American children suffer over the long summer vacation. It is com-mon in American schools—particularly elementary schools—for teachers to spend the first few weeks of each school year reviewing basic skills attained in the previous year.

Over the course of a school career, as much as a year of instructional time is spent on this review process. In foreign countries much less time is needed for this review since the vacation periods are more compressed. This simple school calendar practice, which is embedded in our culture, both places us at a disadvantage in comparing the academic performance of our students with students from abroad and unnecessarily limits the academic attainment of our students.

In this chapter we have looked at a quintet of factors that can greatly affect school performance and yet are below the radar screen of pundits and politi-cal leaders who seek to improve our schools. Most of these factors can best be addressed at the local level. A useful role for the state and federal government would be to buttress these local efforts.

18

International Comparisons

Comparing America's schools to those of other countries requires a level of generalization about our own schools that is at least somewhat questionable. When we look at the great disparities in population, cultures, and wealth across the United States, we need to approach our comparisons and generalizations with a fair degree of humility.

We have some large school districts that are totally populated by students from low socioeconomic backgrounds with all of the disadvantages that such a background implies. We have other students who attend schools in some of the wealthiest communities on the planet. We also have millions of students who attend schools in rural communities with little community pressure to offer a high-powered educational experience for their students.

In per-pupil expenditures alone, there is an incredible disparity among the states. In 2007 Utah spent an average of $5,683 per pupil while New York spent an average of $15,981 per pupil. The average for the United States in 2007 was $9,611 (U.S. Department of Commerce, 2007, xiii).

We should also note that many of the countries that participate in these international comparisons have populations smaller than some of our mid-size cities. Luxembourg, with a population of about half a million for example, is one of the highest performing countries on international tests. The entire student population is on the order of one hundred thousand. This means that the entire nation of Luxembourg is smaller than San Francisco.

Most of these countries also have a far more homogeneous culture than we do in the United States. Nonetheless, school critics often cite international comparisons to bolster their criticisms of America's schools. Reviewing such comparative data, therefore, is both necessary and instructive.

As regularly as the change of the seasons, the Organization for Economic Cooperation and Development (OECD) releases the latest international comparisons on student achievement. The National Center for Education Statistics published a report in 2009 comparing U.S. students' performance in reading, mathematics, and science (Planty et al., 2009).

The reading assessment in 2006 involving forty-five countries showed America's fourth-grade students performing well above average compared with the other forty-four countries. American students ranked eleventh, behind three Canadian provinces, the Russian Federation, Hong Kong, Singapore, Luxembourg, Hungary, Italy, and Sweden. Most of these political entities have very small populations compared with the United States.

The 2007 mathematics comparisons showed U.S. students performing above average at both the fourth- and eighth-grade levels. Fourth-grade students in the United States ranked ninth of thirty-six countries and were surpassed by Hong Kong, Singapore, Chinese Taipei, Japan, Kazakhstan, Russian Federation, England, and Latvia. At the eighth-grade level, American students ranked a respectable sixth of forty-eight countries in the math comparison. They were outranked only by Chinese Taipei, Korea, Singapore, Hong Kong, and Japan.

The 2007 science results showed that American students performed above average at both the fourth- and eighth-grade levels. The good performance of American students at the fourth-grade level was exceeded by only four of the thirty-six participating countries—Singapore, Chinese Taipei, Hong Kong, and Japan. At the eighth-grade level, students ranked tenth of forty-eight countries in science performance. In 2006, however, the average science literacy of fifteen-year-old American students placed them seventeenth of thirty countries in the study.

Taken as a whole, aside from the science performance of fifteen-year-old students, the United States made a very respectable showing. This may explain why the usual hue and cry from politicians and pundits about the crisis in American education was more muted than usual in 2009. More typically, hand-wringing over poor student performance in the United States is followed by garbled analyses of international achievement data coupled with unwarranted recommendations for improving student performance.

Perceived deficiencies are generally attributed to the doleful effects of teachers unions, the lack of proper supervision of instruction, lack of a merit-pay system for teachers, the poor quality of teachers, the length of the school year, poor teacher salaries, and underfunding of the schools. In this chapter we explore some international comparisons on these factors. Some educated assumptions are made in some cases because necessary data are not available for all countries studied.

The analysis is informed by analyzing currently available data, including research from the early 1990s involving six countries (England, Canada, Denmark, Germany, Japan, and the United States), and interviews conducted with a few dozen Fulbright Exchange teachers from these six countries in 1992 (McAdams, 1993). Accessing comparable data in more recent years has reconfirmed some of the comparisons generated in the 1990s.

TEACHER SALARIES

The first comparison concerns the question of teacher salaries in the United States versus other industrialized countries. Conventional opinion for more than fifty years has been that teachers are underpaid, and isn't that regrettable. Proponents of merit pay say that money should be directed toward the best teachers, presumably by transferring some money from the rest of the teaching force. People who argue this way seldom indicate that additional money will be needed to fund these merit-pay plans. The only other reasonable inference is that the proponents assume that so few teachers will receive this merit increase that the effect on school finances will be minimal.

A comparison of average teacher salaries in the United States in the mid-1960s with present day finds that there has been some improvement in teacher pay relative to compensation in the rest of society. This improvement is rather modest, however, since American teachers still earn close to the average income for all workers, not the average for professional personnel. Most people would agree that this is not a particularly impressive statistic.

Comparing teacher salaries across countries is complicated by significant differences in currency values as well as the overall wealth of the different countries. One way to benchmark these comparisons is to take the number of workers in a country and divide this number into the total gross domestic product (GDP) for that country. The quotient for this operation equals the GDP per worker in that country. This number can then be compared with the average teacher salary in each country as a percentage of average GDP per worker.

By this measure we can compare middle school–level teachers across countries with fifteen years of experience as of 2007 (Organization for Economic Cooperation and Development [OECD], 2009, 73). American teachers earn just a bit less than the average worker in the United States. This places them at position twenty-four among the twenty-eight developed countries in the sample in this comparison of average teacher salaries to average worker earnings in the same country. Only teachers in Norway, Sweden, Iceland, and Hungary earn less than U.S. teachers on this measure. Teachers in Switzerland, Germany,

Korea, Portugal, and Mexico earn at least 50 percent more than American teachers on this measure.

Another way of looking at the question of comparative teacher salaries is to relate the salary to the average GDP per capita in each country surveyed. By this measure American teachers with fifteen years experience earn 96 percent of the average GDP per capita, while the average for all countries surveyed is 117 percent. In Korea, the average teacher at this experience level earns 221 percent of the country's GDP per capita.

TEACHER WORKING CONDITIONS

Those public school critics who would find these data defensible would be quick to argue that American teachers have a relatively easy lifestyle. They only work seven-hour days, and they enjoy a three-month vacation each year. A closer look at actual data on teacher working conditions here and abroad offers some surprising information. Research in the 1990s found that teachers in other countries often have a shorter workday than American teachers. They have few if any supervisory responsibilities toward students outside the classroom. They have fewer hours of direct instruction to students during the school week. They also experience more overall job satisfaction than do American teachers.

The Fulbright teachers interviewed in the 1990s who worked for a year in American schools were shocked at the workload and intensity of the daily schedule for American teachers. These Fulbright teachers were reporting on their experiences in school districts in every part of the United States (McAdams, 1993). The daily work life of American teachers has certainly not improved over the intervening years.

Elementary school teachers in all countries spend a larger proportion of their time providing direct instruction than do their secondary school counterparts. The difference is slight in the United States where elementary teachers spend somewhat more than 80 percent of their time in direct instruction. Looking at schools abroad, we find that elementary teachers elsewhere, on average, spend about 45 percent of their time in direct instruction. Foreign exchange teachers interviewed in the 1990s were virtually unanimous in their amazement at the difficult and grueling daily schedules that they found in the American schools where they spent one year as exchange teachers.

The 2009 report *Highlights From Education at a Glance*, which compares annual teaching hours in twenty-six countries, reveals that teachers in the United States spend almost 1,100 hours per year formally on the job. The average for these twenty-eight countries is between seven hundred and eight hundred hours. American teachers spend many more hours on duty than their counterparts in other highly industrialized countries in Europe and in Japan (OECD, 2009, 75). This is in spite of the fact that American critics of public education say that one cure for our perceived deficiencies would be a longer school year.

How is it possible that we have a shorter school year than most countries and yet our teachers and students spend more time in formal instruction than their counterparts in these same countries? The reason is that although students and teachers may attend school for more days in other countries, the school days are typically shorter. Many other countries also schedule more short breaks for teachers and students during the school day than is true in the United States. American schools, particularly secondary schools, allow only a few minutes between classes for students to walk from class to class, with the school day as a whole proceeding in lockstep at a frenetic pace.

Schools in England, for example, have a time set aside in mid-morning for morning tea, where both teachers and students have fifteen to twenty minutes to take a break from formal instruction. Perhaps we should have a longer school year in the United States, but perhaps we should also use these extra days to slow down the pace. This might be a situation where less is more in terms of productive instructional time within a given school day.

Another interesting datum from this study relates to average class sizes in the United States versus other countries. The average class size at the primary school level for U.S. teachers is twenty-two, while the average for all twenty-eight countries in the study is about twenty-one. The average class size in American schools at the lower secondary level is twenty-five, just slightly above the average of twenty-four for the twenty-four countries in the study. The average class size ranges from thirty-five in Korea to eighteen in Luxembourg. Thus, on this measure, the situation for American teachers is similar to the norm worldwide (OECD, 2009, 70–71).

Contact time with students as a proportion of workload for teachers provides another interesting comparison of American teachers versus their peers abroad. American secondary teachers spend about 70 to 80 percent of their workday in actual interaction with students. The average for the fifteen countries cited in the *Education at a Glance* study is about 30 to 40 percent of the workday. Japanese secondary school teachers, for example, spend only about one quarter of their workday providing direct instruction to students (OECD, 2009, 75).

IMPACT OF TEACHERS UNIONS

The negative impact of teachers unions is another favorite target of school critics. When we look at teachers in foreign countries we find that most other countries have teacher associations or unions, some more militant than others.

The argument is that teachers unions impede proper supervision practices by school administrators. In exploring teacher supervision practices abroad, we find that few countries have a vigorous teacher supervision and evaluation process. Some summary statements from the *Highlights From Education at a Glance 2009* encapsulate the state of teacher supervision on an international basis (OECD, 2009, 82).

- "A third or more of teachers in Austria, Ireland and Portugal worked in schools whose principal reported no internal or external school evaluations in the past five years."
- "Teachers' appraisal and feedback are rarely associated with material incentives, and in most countries they are not substantially linked either to financial benefits or career advancement. Across all countries, just nine percent of teachers reported that appraisal or feedback had a moderate or large impact upon their salary."

On the question of whether or not poor performance was punished, the study noted the following:

Did teachers think that poor teaching was being punished? . . . The answer was broadly no: In most countries most teachers reported that sustained poor performance would not lead to dismissal, while more than three-quarters of the teachers reported that their principal did not take steps to alter the monetary awards of persistently underperforming teachers.

This is not to say that a lack of evaluation of teachers is a good thing, but merely that perfunctory supervision practices are the norm. We can conclude that in countries that outperform the United States in international testing, the good results cannot be attributed to close supervision of their teachers. Remember that the usual context of this discussion is by school critics who imply that the lack of merit pay is a reason for the perceived underperformance of American students relative to students in other countries.

Merit pay is yet another proposed solution to improve teaching in America's schools. Here again we look in vain to teaching practices in foreign countries that would support the notion that merit pay is a viable and desirable option for teacher compensation. Most other countries have salary schedules similar to those in American schools. Like our schools, foreign schools are not staffed administratively to implement the supervisory rigor that a merit-pay system implies.

Unions are thought by some to bear a responsibility for perceived high salaries and easy working conditions for teachers. If this is the goal of American teachers unions, we can conclude from these data that unions have not materially improved teacher compensation in America over the years. One could argue, of course, that teacher salaries would be even lower in the absence of unions. It is safe to predict that the advantages that teachers currently enjoy in the area of benefits compared to private-sector employees will decline significantly over the next decade.

Salaries of American teachers are not competitive with teacher salaries in most other highly developed countries. Furthermore, teacher working conditions in the United States are far more onerous than that of teachers abroad. Collective bargaining has not materially improved the daily work life of the typical teacher after more than forty years of contract negotiations.

Two areas of teacher compensation that may owe some credit to the unions are the level of fringe benefits for teachers relative to those enjoyed by the general population, and pensions that are far superior to those of private-sector workers. In these respects teachers enjoy similar advantages in benefits and pensions as that of other public employees. The rich benefits programs for public employees relative to the private sector are coming under increasing scrutiny by the general public facing local and state revenue shortfalls and tax increases.

Another interesting comparison of schools across cultures is the amount of class time lost to student inattentiveness and misbehavior. Studies from around the world indicate that classroom climate is one of the most important predictors of student achievement. In the Teaching and Learning International Survey, teachers were asked about the percentage of time that they spend on actual instruction, otherwise known as *time on task*.

On average, teachers in the twenty-three countries in the survey reported spending about 10–15 percent of their time on keeping order in the classroom (OECD, 2009, 84–85). Unfortunately, the United States did not participate in this survey. From hundreds of classroom observation of classes over forty years, however, the 10 percent figure seems to be a reasonable estimate for the typical American classroom.

The problem in America is that in schools where discipline is bad, it tends to be very bad. This is a major problem in too many schools in the urban cores of our major cities. The 10 percent estimate for time spent on classroom management is typical in about 75 percent of our classrooms nationwide, but is often far higher in the other 25 percent of our schools.

ATTRACTING AND RETAINING TEACHERS

Attracting and retaining qualified and effective teachers is a constant concern of educational policy makers in the United States. The problem is always particularly acute in hard-to-staff subjects such as mathematics, science, and foreign languages. An OECD report, *Teachers Matter: Attracting, Developing and Retaining Effective Teachers*, reveals that these issues are of critical concern in countries throughout the world.

The study, involving twenty-five countries including the United States, identified the following major concerns (OECD, 2005, 1–5):

- About half the countries report serious concerns about maintaining an adequate supply of good quality teachers, especially in high-demand subject areas.
- There are concerns about the image and status of teaching, and teachers often feel that their work is undervalued.
- Teachers' relative salaries are declining in most countries.
- Almost all countries report concerns about "qualitative" shortfalls: whether enough teachers have the knowledge and skills to meet school needs.
- Some countries experience high rates of teacher attrition, especially among new teachers.
- Teachers express concerns about the effects of high workloads, stress, and poor working environments on job satisfaction and teaching effectiveness.
- Processes for responding to ineffective teaching are often cumbersome and slow.

These international concerns are virtually identical to criticisms of America schools and teachers over the past forty years. Although these issues are critical concerns in the United States, perhaps we can gain some perspective by the fact that these problems are not unique to our country.

FINANCING THE SCHOOLS

The one area where America's schools diverge sharply from most countries is the method by which schools are financed. We have seen that in the United States the state and local governments primarily finance education. States vary widely in the proportion of funding provided at the local versus the state level. One state, Hawaii, has only one school district and thus education there is funded totally at the state level. Other states provide from one-third to two-thirds of the funding.

There is no question, however, that the United States relies on local funding to a far larger extent than do other countries. The *Education at a Glance 2008* report indicates clearly that the United States is out of the mainstream with respect to educational funding by the various levels of government. On average, the thirty OECD countries provide 46 percent of school funding from the national level, 27 percent at the regional level, and 27 percent at the local level. The United States provides 10 percent of funding nationally, 39 percent regionally (states), and 51 percent locally (OECD, Indicator B4).

Most other developed countries ensure greater equity in school financing than is found in the United States. In addition, the smaller proportion of funds raised locally in most countries avoids much of the contentiousness about school finances that is so common in American communities. In the United States school boards and or other local governments engage in yearly arguments over the proper level of school funding. These recurring disagreements in America's local communities over school funding are an ongoing impediment to community cohesion regarding support for the schools.

Another major point of contention in the United States concerns financial support for nonpublic schools. Our country has a long-standing practice of denying public funds for nonpublic schools because of constitutional issues. The closest we come to financing nonpublic schools involve a small number of voucher programs serving about 170,000 students nationally.

Many people mistakenly think of charter schools as nonpublic schools. Strictly speaking, however, charter schools are publicly funded schools without many of the requirements placed on typical public schools. Charter schools are particularly popular alternatives to some of our dysfunctional schools in our inner cities.

SECONDARY SCHOOL EXIT EXAMS

The last comparison concerns the concept of exit exams for students finishing secondary school. This is truly a foreign concept in the United States. The closest analogs we have to a national exit exam in the United States are the American College Test (ACT) and the Scholastic Aptitude Test (SAT) college entrance tests. Unfortunately, these are not true achievement tests but rather are designed as measures of how a student is likely to perform in his or her first year of college.

A detailed study of external exit exams in several other countries (England and Wales, France, Germany, and Japan) reveals a dramatically different approach to educational accountability than is typical in the United States. These foreign countries use external exit exams both to certify that students have reached a satisfactory level of educational achievement and as a screening device for admission to higher education (Eckstein, 1994, 1–12).

Years ago these foreign countries used these exams primarily as a way to allocate limited spaces in higher education to the most accomplished students. This approach is inimical to our social values in the United States, a fact that accounts for our traditional opposition to such exit exams. This aspect of exit exams in foreign countries has changed dramatically over the past few decades.

Today almost all highly developed countries have greatly expanded access to higher education and have provided alternate routes to higher education to students who do not perform well as secondary school students. These tests do provide an objective measure of actual individual student academic achievement and they indirectly reflect on the schools that the students attend.

We have no such objective measure of academic achievement for individual students on a nationwide basis. Over the past thirty years, there have been sporadic attempts among about one-half of the states to implement exit exams for high school students. In most cases these exams caused political controversy to such an extent that most states discontinued the exam. The controversies generally centered on the propensity for these exams to have a differential impact on students from different races. Today about one-half of the states either have exit exams or plan to require them in the near future.

America's approach to academic standards and accountability has focused on the school rather than the student. Placing more of the onus for achievement and graduation on individual students would provide the motivation for more students to perform at a higher level. Mandated exit exams would also subtly change the relationship between students and teachers in American schools.

Presently American teachers are seen as a hurdle to student acceptance to colleges since admissions are highly reliant on high school grades. Thus both the student and his parents can view a teacher as an umpire and an obstacle. In countries with rigorous exit exams, the teacher is often viewed as a coach—one who assists the student in satisfactorily passing the national or regional exams.

Another interesting difference between high-stakes testing in the United States and many foreign countries involves the nature of the tests. Our SAT tests and state assessments of basic skills rely almost totally on multiple-choice and true-false tests. This is also true for the more recent state exit exams. Many other nations require oral presentations or written, essay-type answers.

These types of assessments require higher-order thinking skills and greater clarity of expression than are required with multiple choice–type tests. These more elaborate testing practices in some foreign countries obviously imply a far higher level of financial and time investments on the part of schools to implement them successfully.

Throughout this chapter, we have explored many similar comparative practices and realities that are common to most nations. Examples of these similarities include concerns about attracting and retaining teachers, the rela-tively low salary and status of teachers across nations, and the lack of close supervision or merit-pay practices in most nations. Other similarities include class size practices, student discipline practices, single salary schedules, and the prevalence of teachers unions and associations.

Notable differences between foreign schools and American schools exist in several areas. American schools are funded in a much less equitable manner than in most foreign countries. The school year is shorter in the United States than in many countries, although actual instruction time over the course of a year is actually greater than the international norm.

The teacher workday in the United States is much more frenetic and in-cludes a far higher proportion of available time in direct instruction than is common elsewhere. Other nations are far more likely to provide public financing for nonpublic schools than is permissible under our Constitution. External secondary school exit exams are almost universal in foreign nations while true high-stakes exit exams are still uncommon in the United States.

In the next and final chapter, we revisit some of the more fruitful practices in foreign countries such as the nature of the school calendar and exit exams from secondary school. We discuss how these practices might be modified for use in the United States.

19

Final Exam

$\textbf{A}$ good final exam in essay form requires the student to summarize, analyze, and synthesize the content of the course and to identify a few major themes from the instructional exercise. One major purpose of this book is to provide some flavor of the context in which American schools operate. The chapters on teachers, parents, administrators, and school board members each demonstrate that our schools interact with large swaths of the general public on a daily basis.

We have reviewed the actual operation of the schools from the vantage point of teachers, administrators, and school board members. We have highlighted the strengths of our schools as well as their deficiencies. We have critiqued some of the common proposals for improving the schools and demonstrated why most of the solutions suggested are either impractical or insufficient.

FAULTY IMPROVEMENT STRATEGIES

Before summarizing strategies for improving those of our schools that are underperforming, we should reiterate some reasons why the most frequently discussed ideas for school reform are either impractical or politically impossible. Merit pay is a prime example of an idea that is both impractical and politically unrealistic.

Other nations identified by school critics as superior to America's schools do not have merit-pay systems. Even if desirable, the existing political influence that teachers unions have with state legislatures and governors would need to be greatly diminished before meaningful merit-pay legislation could be passed.

Also, significantly more funds would be required administratively to implement the intensive supervision program that a merit-pay system implies.

Diminishing the power of teachers unions is another proposal that is simply unattainable from a political standpoint. In many states teachers unions are the most powerful lobby and contribute the most money and exert the greatest political pressure on legislatures and school boards. Whether or not checking the influence of teachers unions is desirable, it is not going to happen as a practical matter. There would need to be a much higher level of public concern about schools before legislators would feel empowered to curtail the power of teachers unions.

Increasing the length of the school year is another popular proposal offering less than meets the eye. Other countries have 200 to 210 school days per year compared with our 180. A closer examination of school routines in many foreign countries, however, reveals that the school day is often shorter than in the United States or the proportion of available time for academics is less than in the United States. Financing an increased school year would also be problematic, given that we struggle to finance the 180-day school year that we already have.

Charter schools and school vouchers are other popular panaceas that will have only limited impact on a national scale. In many parts of the country, such alternatives are impractical because the geographic size of districts would necessitate very long bus rides that would be unacceptable to both parents and students. Also, in many areas parents are quite satisfied with their public school—in some cases more satisfied than they should be.

In an excellent public school district in a Philadelphia suburb only seven students attend a charter school, whereas 3,600 attend the public school. In fairness, about two thousand students attend various private schools in this very affluent community. On the other hand, in a much lower-performing school district of 7,200 public school students in suburban Philadelphia, almost 1,500 additional students attend charter schools. Charter schools are a welcome alternative for parents with students attending underperforming schools, but they are not a realistic solution to the deficiencies of poorly performing schools in many areas of the country. Many charter schools are not effective and far stronger oversight is needed if these schools are to thrive.

CHANGING STUDENT DEMOGRAPHICS— EXISTING AND POTENTIAL STRATEGIES

A principal challenge facing American schools is the changing demographics of the student body and the accompanying complications of providing a quality educational experience. As the decades have passed, the public school population consists of an ever-larger proportion of students from socioeconomically deprived communities who often have minimal skills as English speakers. Many supports such as Title I remedial assistance and English language learner programs have ameliorated these challenges, but not sufficiently to overcome the demographic challenges.

Most other highly developed countries have much smaller immigrant and minority cultural groups to assimilate into the schools. A more homogeneous society and culture greatly simplify the task of the schools. The poor educational performance of our American underclass, besides being a moral disgrace in its own right, represents a mortal danger to the future health of American society.

The substantial minority of our students from troubled homes and disintegrating communities naturally lead to underperforming schools. The charter school movement represents a welcome lifeline to those parents who can access these schools, but they are not the ultimate solution to the problem.

There is some irony in the fact that forty-five years ago disruptive and uncooperative students were removed from the public schools, whereas today we separate the conscientious students from the public schools via charter schools. This leaves a higher proportion of the less conscientious and more disruptive students behind in the regular public schools—exacerbating an already intractable problem.

This dynamic will ultimately be unsustainable because as charter schools expand in number and student capacity, they necessarily will be reaching deeper into the pool of available students, tapping into a greater number of unmotivated students and their disengaged parents. These are the very students and parents that are the bane of our existing dysfunctional schools.

The noted educational historian and scholar Diane Ravitch, an early advocate of charter schools, has changed her mind about their efficacy. She served as assistant secretary of education from 1991 to 1993 under the George H. W. Bush administration. During and after her tenure at the Department of Education, she was a strong advocate for charter schools as a means to bring needed competition to our public school system. Almost twenty years later she has changed her opinion about charter schools.

Ravitch provides a rationale for her change of heart in a March 9, 2010, article in *The Wall Street Journal*. Citing studies on charter schools, she reports that they vary widely in quality. Reporting on the only major national evaluation of charter schools funded by pro–charter school foundations, she notes that the study found that "compared to regular public schools, 17 percent of charters got higher test scores, 46 percent had gains that were no different from their public counterparts, and 37 percent were significantly worse off" (Ravitch, 2010).

Ravitch reports that "charter evaluations frequently note that as compared to neighboring public schools, charters enroll smaller proportions of students whose English is limited and students with disabilities. The students who are hardest to educate are left to regular public schools." On graduation rates for charter schools, Ravitch reports, "The higher graduation rate posted by charters often reflects the fact that they are able to 'counsel out' the lowest performing students; many charters have very high attrition rates (in some, 50%–60% of those who start fall away)."

A more systemic approach to the problems of dysfunctional communities needs to be developed if the millions of our severely disadvantaged students are to be saved. Geoffrey Canada, CEO of the Harlem Children's Zone, has developed just such an innovative approach to school reform in the heart of Harlem. The *New York Times Magazine* in an article on June 24, 2004, declared this program as "one of the most ambitious social experiments of our time" (Tough, 2004). The Harlem Children's Zone Project was launched in 1997 as a program to deliver a comprehensive range of services to an entire Harlem community. Today the project covers one hundred city blocks and serves over seventeen thousand children.

This same article said the Harlem Zone Project "combines educational, social and medical services. It starts at birth and follows children to college. It meshes those services into an interlocking web, and then it drops that web over an entire neighborhood. . . . The objective is to create a safety net woven so tightly that children in the neighborhood just can't slip through" (Tough, 2009). To extend programs such as the Harlem Children's Zone to the hundreds of communities that require such an intense approach would represent a truly comprehensive solution.

As a charter school, the Harlem Children's Zone receives the same instructional cost per student as is spent in regular New York City public schools. More than half of the budget for the program, however, is provided by private funds. This degree of private funding is not available on a system-wide basis. We need a domestic version of the Marshall Plan that brought about the recovery of European economies after the devastation of World War II. Although the cost would be tremendous, we simply cannot afford to cripple the future of 25 to 30 percent of America's children.

In the past we have tried to tweak the system to improve inner-city schools. The problems are much too critical to continue with a "rearranging the deck chairs on the *Titanic*" approach. Even the Obama administration's $5.8 billion Challenge Grants represent less than 1 percent of the funds spent on public education annually in this country. Too many of our children live in dysfunctional communities, and the failure of the schools in these communities is but one symptom of the deeper problem. Successful charter schools have proven that students from inner-city environments can succeed academi-cally, but much greater social supports need to be in place for such successes to occur on a community-wide basis.

The very radical approach of actually removing students from their homes and communities, as well as their schools, has been successful in Washing-ton, D.C. The SEED Charter School is a residential school that is in many ways comparable to the boarding schools attended by the children of our elites. The school has an enrollment of 320 students in grades 6–12, and operates an academically rigorous college preparatory program. The cost per student in 2006 was $33,000 (Office of Innovation and Improvement, 2006, 55–58). The operating budget of almost $13 million in 2010 translates to a per-pupil expenditure of approximately $40,000.

As a charter school, SEED receives a per-pupil allocation from the city, but this accounts for only a small part of its revenue. Most of the school's revenue comes from government grants as well as individual and corporate gifts. At $40,000 per pupil, this model is obviously not viable as a large-scale solution to the problems of our dysfunctional schools. It may, however, lead to consideration of other less-costly strategies to remove students from toxic environments to the greatest extent possible.

There have been hundreds of examples where students in charter schools or academies financed by philanthropists have enjoyed impressive academic achievement. The critical difference between students in these schools and the general population of students is the commitment of the parents to support their children's academic progress. Many of these schools insist that parents sign contracts regarding parental participation in support of the schools. Once a school has a critical mass of students and parents dedicated to academic achievement, the culture of the school begins to reinforce achievement rather than mitigate against achievement, as is common in dysfunctional schools lacking parental support.

If charter schools are not the ultimate answer, what can be done to improve the education in many of our urban schools? Most cities remove the truly criminally dangerous students from the regular public school and have them attend small schools that are very highly structured. There is another category of students, however—those who are disengaged and disruptive, but not dan-gerously so. These students have poor attendance records, fail most of their classes, and often interfere with good order in the classroom. These students fail year after year until they finally drop out. The dropout rate in many of our most troubled urban school districts is about 50 percent.

We need to try something different with these disengaged students. Per-haps a small number of theme schools, concentrating on some of the work skills and content found in traditional technical schools, could be available in neighborhoods throughout the city. These small schools should have an enrollment of only about two hundred students. Students unable to deal with the structure and expectations of the regular middle or high school could be assigned to attend one of these theme schools. If the student is unsuccessful in the first assigned school, he or she should have the opportunity to try one or more of the others. This initiative will provide opportunity for these students to have a fresh start in a context where many more of them will succeed.

As a corollary benefit, the regular school would have fewer disengaged students who are disruptive and unsuccessful. The remaining students, who are able to cope in the larger school academic environment, will find themselves in a school with higher academic standards and a more businesslike learning environment. These students will experience more academic growth, as will the students in the small theme schools. Teacher job satisfaction will improve in the regular public school, leading to a higher level of performance and a lower level of teacher turnover from year to year.

The less-than-stellar performance of American students on some international comparisons of student achievement is largely a function of the 25 percent of our student population who attend failing schools in fractured communities. The admittedly expensive and comprehensive solutions for this problem would themselves lead to an improvement in overall student performance on international achievement tests. More importantly, millions of our young people would be saved from lives of poverty and despair.

In spite of the challenges schools face because of a changing demographic over the years, there has been some improvement in the performance of minority students over the past few decades (Rampey, Dion, and Donahue, 2009, 4). These small improvements have come with great effort and even greater economic costs to our society. We should appreciate the small successes we have enjoyed given a continuing deterioration in the socioeconomic realities facing so many of our school communities.

In the following paragraphs we briefly explore initiatives, many at little cost, that could significantly increase academic achievement for students in all public schools. The items are listed from the least costly to the more costly recommendations.

MAXIMIZING THE POWER OF HOMEWORK

Properly conceived, homework assignments can extend the student's learning through practice of skills learned in class and extend the breadth of the knowledge first presented in a classroom setting. If currently disengaged students could be inspired to spend even one hour on homework per school night, they would gain the equivalent of two extra years of educational skill development and knowledge acquisition by the time they graduate from high school. Should we be surprised that more diligent students perform better academically? Our best-performing school districts nationwide already incorporate suitable homework assignments as a critical part of their academic program.

RAISING PARENTAL EXPECTATIONS

A low-cost method to improve student achievement involves educating more parents toward valuing education and therefore expecting a higher level of academic performance by their children. From a national perspective, only about one-third of parents today are sufficiently concerned about the academic achievement of their children to insist on high academic performance. Teachers would applaud the more active engagement of parents in support of schools with higher academic standards and expectations.

Too many parents are still in a time warp where they subconsciously believe that their children will have good job prospects simply because they live in the United States. This is no longer the case. If our politicians and opinion leaders can find a way to convince parents that a good education is critical to the welfare of their children, better achievement will surely follow.

Critics of public education constantly chant the mantra that we need better teachers. This would obviously help. What we really need, however, are better students. Better students means students who actually come to school, go to classes, and give their attention to academic work. Such students would do their homework and study for their tests. As stated previously, about one-third of parents already encourage and insist that their children behave in this manner. If even another one-third of parents could be convinced that good academic performance is critical to their child's success, there would be dramatic improvement in test scores to the benefit of individual students and society as a whole.

RECONFIGURING THE SCHOOL CALENDAR

Although not a new idea, changing our annual school calendar toward shorter summer vacations and more breaks within the school year would lead to some improvement in achievement. The reluctance of American schools to implement a revised school calendar owes more to cultural inertia than to any valid reason to maintain our current schedule. These scheduling initiatives would probably need to be initiated at the state level because school boards and superintendents attempting such changes at the local district level would experience significant resistance from parents and teachers.

POSITIVELY IMPACTING SCHOOL CULTURE

The importance of the culture of a school was discussed in the chapter on schools as organizations. Successful charter schools create a new culture of achievement and mutual respect for those students and parents who elect to attend these schools. There is, however, a culture of poverty that afflicts people over several generations and immobilizes many of them even if their material conditions are improved. Cultural change needs to be embedded in the wider community to reinforce positive cultural changes in the schools.

There are always a number of persons who can rise above their surroundings through determination and grit. The challenge is to improve the general culture for the majority of people living in a disadvantaged environment. The effects of the culture on a group of people are so pervasive, however, that their influence is often obscured. How, for example, can we overcome the prevailing thinking among young black males in our inner cities that to achieve well in schools is "acting white"? Powerful peer pressure is applied to young black students who would like to achieve well in school, but who submit to the negative influences of their peer group.

A good example of the hidden effects of school cultures concerns the dramatic differences in academic achievement between boys and girls. The *Washington Times* reported on April 20, 2006, that a Manhattan Institute study found that one-third of boys failed to graduate from high school compared with a 72 percent graduation rate for girls. The gender gap was greatest among minority students, with less than one-half of black and Hispanic boys graduating from high school compared with a graduation rate of 60 percent for minority females ("Third of boys," 2006).

This disparity becomes even greater when the gender breakdown for college graduates is considered. The *Wall Street Journal* presented the following data in its February 12, 2010, issue: women earn 135 bachelor's degrees for every 100 earned by men. The disparity among minority young adults is substantially greater. Black women are earning 192 bachelor's degrees for every 100 earned by black men (McQueen, 2010).

The relevance of this data to school cultures is apparent. For some reason, girls are more likely to thrive in the school environment than are boys. The staffing ratio of women to men in public schools has always been about three to one. It should not be surprising that schools generally reflect feminine sensibilities. Schools have always been less appealing to the male psyche.

In the past, the great majority of school administrators were men. Perhaps they had a counterbalancing effect by influencing the practices and culture of the school toward a more centered position along the masculine-feminine continuum. In the past two decades many more women have joined the administrative ranks, entrenching the female perspective in both the classrooms and the administrative offices. This is a cultural phenomenon not likely to be noticed by the school staff. This could be a case where a feminized zeitgeist in the schools is so pervasive that it is not easily perceived.

If this notion of overly feminized schools as a factor in lower male achievement rates is true, this should be a relatively easy problem to remediate. There have been many initiatives in recent decades to improve female college attendance rates and female participation in higher-level math and science courses. Perhaps it is time for a similar effort to improve the academic standing of males. If such a change were to occur, this alone would lift graduation rates and the performance level of schools both nationally and in international comparisons.

Schools with a positive culture are characterized by a relaxed yet businesslike learning environment. Students attend regularly and come to class on time. They complete out-of-class assignments and participate in class activities. A school with such characteristics makes it possible for teachers to be effective instructors. Teachers exhibit positive morale that is contagious among students and staff alike.

An effective principal will do everything in his or her power to nourish such a learning climate. Settling for low standards for student behavior and teacher performance will undermine any possibility for developing a positive school culture. Demanding such a positive climate in our schools will itself lead to better student achievement.

CURRICULUM STANDARDS AND CURRICULUM AUDITING

Development of a rigorous and fairly uniform curriculum across major academic subject areas would have significant positive effects on achievement. These curricula should be aligned both with the National Assessment of Educational Progress and the major international tests that involve American students. If a national curriculum proves politically impossible, the states should commit themselves to curriculum in major academic areas that are as closely aligned among states as possible.

We saw in chapter 12, "School Boards," that local school boards cannot reasonably be expected to effectively create or monitor curriculum. We also saw in chapter 14, "The Critical Role of the School Principal," that supervision of teachers is done in a perfunctory manner, if at all, in many school districts.

Properly monitoring the implementation of the curriculum will require a much more serious effort than current practice allows. The state should be responsible for monitoring the implementation of curricula with the same rigor that most states employ to monitor school finances.

A cadre of county or regional curriculum specialists should be assigned to audit the curriculum. A team of such experts should visit every school a few times each year. Teacher lesson plans should be examined as well as teacher-created tests. Students could be interviewed to further ensure that the major elements of the curriculum are being taught to students. The principal would be responsible for evaluating the teacher on instructional techniques, as well as all other elements characteristic of effective teaching. The regional experts should provide the principal and superintendent with a report on compliance with the curriculum and it would be the responsibility of the principal to take remedial action when required.

EXIT EXAMS

In chapter 18, "International Comparisons," we saw that many foreign countries administer regional or national exit exams to secondary students. In most cases these are high-stakes tests—they determine whether or not the student graduates and determine whether or where the student will attend a college or university. This common requirement internationally fixes accountability on both students and schools in an objective manner. These exit exams extend beyond basic reading and math and include tests in several other basic subjects.

Such high-stakes exit exams could only be implemented if the state ensures that all students are exposed to and given an opportunity to master the curriculum content to be tested. This factor reinforces the importance of monitoring curriculum compliance at the local level by state officials. The construction, administration, and grading of such exit exams is an appropriate task for state-level education agencies. The test results themselves will also be good indicators of the extent of curriculum compliance in a given school district.

The relationship between teachers and students in an exit test environment becomes that of a mentor to a student. In the United States, students rely heavily on teacher-awarded grades to compete for admission to competitive colleges. This emphasis on high school grades often places teachers under great pressure from parents, students, and school officials to award higher grades than may be justifiable. With an external objective standard of performance, teachers would assign grades based on the extent to which the student is making progress toward preparing for the mandatory exit exams.

Some states have attempted exit exams, only to find public objections as too many students fail to pass the tests. Many states have previously mandated exit exams, only to repeal the requirement in the face of political pressures. About one-half of our states now require or plan to implement exit examinations. Such exit exams ideally will go beyond testing in reading and mathematics.

All high school graduates should be able to display at least a basic understanding of our system of government, our history, world cultures, and geography, and sufficient facility with the written and spoken word to communicate at a reasonable level of sophistication. These testing requirements will succeed only if there is the political will to impose real performance standards rather than lower or remove the standard due to political pressure.

Current state assessments generally report student and school performance but imply no consequences for students. Poor schoolwide performance is seen as reflecting badly on the school with no consideration of the extent to which poor performance reflects on individual students and their parents. After thirty years of experience with publishing test results in the local press, we have seen little outcry from the public to improve the academic rigor of local schools.

Perhaps there is a subtle understanding by the public that these results are driven as much by individual student deficiencies as they are by failures of the schools and teachers. It is easier for a politician to blame the schools, however, than to suggest that part of the blame lies with the parents and their children.

Before leaving the issue of the role of students in their own education, we must briefly explore the cultural context in which students live their lives. There once was a time when schools represented the major influence on a student aside from their home and perhaps their church. The pull of the general culture is much more influential on the attitudes and interests of children than was true forty years ago, and certainly more than sixty years ago at the dawn of the television age.

Educators have for decades urged parents to guide their children to spend a greater proportion of their time in academic pursuits as opposed to passive experiences such as watching TV and movies, playing video games, and listening to popular music. These efforts have largely been ineffective as the pull of these media have become even greater over the years.

A breakdown of time spent on education versus other activities is instructive. Assuming that a child sleeps for eight hours a day, this leaves about 110 hours in a week for other experiences. Over a fifty-two-week period, this total of waking hours exceeds 5,500. Assuming that a student spends six hours per day in school, for 180 days per year, the total time under the influence of a formal education is about 1,100. This represents only 20 percent of a student's waking hours! How reasonable is it to ascribe any deficiencies in our students, academic and otherwise, solely to underperforming schools and teachers?

THE TEACHER FACTOR

It is fitting to end this book as we began it—with the teacher. What about the issue of attracting and retaining a better cadre of teachers? The usual panaceas of merit pay, intensive supervision, dismissal of bad teachers, or curbing teachers union power do not appear to be features of the foreign school systems that school critics point to as exemplars. In any event, such proposed changes are difficult to achieve as a practical matter.

Teacher organizations are often the most effective lobby in state legislatures and there is simply no appetite for diminishing union power even if such a change were desirable. Merit-pay plans cannot be implemented because the financial resources necessary to administer such a system are not available. The time and energy necessary to dismiss teachers under current legal constraints can, except in the most egregious cases, be better spent in improving the training and performance of the general teaching force.

The *Wall Street Journal* of February 22, 2010, reported that the Los Angeles School District recently spent $3.5 million trying to dismiss seven teachers ("No [Tenured] Teacher," 2010). Four were ultimately dismissed or resigned, but a few were reinstated. This district spent an average of $500,000 per teacher over a five-year period but was successful only half the time. It is the responsibility of state legislatures to modify the tenure laws so that it is easier and far less costly to dismiss incompetent teachers. Until such changes are made in the state legislatures, local school districts need to be very careful about expending the time and money necessary to attempt to dismiss a teacher under current conditions.

The one area in which the teaching cadre could be improved is by recruiting the best available candidates as entry-level teachers. There are many young people who could be very good teachers, but do not enter the profession because of low entry-level salaries. The typical twenty-two-year-old college graduate is more than $20,000 in debt from college loans and is trying to establish himself or herself as an independent adult—a difficult transition in today's economy. Teaching has very good health benefits and pension benefits when compared with other professions, but these enticements are of minimal importance to a young person beginning his or her career.

Let us assume that beginning teacher salaries need to increase by about $10,000 to bring better-prepared students into the applicant pool. This does not mean that all teacher salaries need to increase by this amount, or at all in some cases. On a standard salary schedule, this increase in starting salaries could be melded into the existing salary schedule. There could be large increases at the beginning step, and gradually decrease in magnitude at higher salary steps, until they meld into the existing schedule, perhaps at step 10 or so.

This procedure implies an average of a $5,000 increase for teachers at the lower one-third of the experience level. This would impact about one million teachers nationally for an annual cost of $5 billion. This is a large figure, but still represents the amount that the Obama administration is allocating for Challenge Grants. A salary increase for beginning teachers would have a much more potent long-term positive effect on education than the new grant initiatives that come and go with each new state and federal administration.

If additional monies were to be provided for beginning teachers, it is critical that the funds be allocated as direct grants from the state or federal government to individual teachers. These grants could be $10,000 for first-year teachers, $9,000 for second-year teachers, and so on until by the tenth year the teacher's total salary would be determined by the local salary schedule with no additional grants from the state or federal government. This approach is essential because if the funds were given directly to the district, they would end up being distributed within a salary schedule at the local level as determined through negotiations with the teachers union.

Political power within a teachers union is generally concentrated in mid-career teachers who are officers and negotiators in these organizations. These teacher representatives quite naturally view the distribution of monies within a salary schedule through the lens of their own self-interest. They tend to believe that they should use the district's natural interest in increasing starting salaries as a lever to finance similar increases throughout the salary scale. School boards are typically insufficiently concerned with how monies are distributed within a salary schedule and more concerned with the total cost of the settlement.

Over the years this dynamic has allocated available funds toward the middle and top of teacher salary schedules. Teachers could defend this common practice by noting that even with these pressures to concentrate money at the middle to top of the salary schedule, teacher salaries relative to other workers have changed little over the past forty years—in spite of whatever pressures that union negotiations may exert on school budgets.

Another possibility is to provide federal funds to substantially increase the salaries of teachers working in urban school districts. A $10,000 increase in the salaries of all inner-city teachers would cost between $5 and $10 billion per year. This is certainly a substantial sum of money, although it represents only about 1 percent of total spending on K–12 education in the United States.

Another possibility is to initiate a more robust loan forgiveness program for teachers. These programs have existed for some time and are designed to attract teachers to the more challenging school districts by forgiving college loans over a ten-year period. Applying eligibility for these programs to a higher proportion of districts and shortening the total loan forgiveness period from ten to five years should attract more young teachers to the profession.

A potent approach to retaining teachers in the profession is to improve the work life of the teacher. More parental involvement, external exit tests requiring solid achievement standards, and the ability to remove disruptive students from our regular public schools would all contribute to a change in the culture of schools toward a more academic orientation. This would greatly improve teacher morale and job satisfaction that then would encourage a virtuous cycle between teachers and students to the benefit of student achievement.

We saw in chapter 18, "International Comparisons," that American teachers spend considerably more time in direct student contact as compared with teachers in most other nations. Unfortunately, to address this issue would either require more teachers or larger class sizes. Larger class sizes would be counterproductive and not politically feasible. Hiring a substantial number of additional teachers is not financially viable.

Furthermore, we are currently unable to find enough certified and qualified teachers to staff our schools at the existing size of our teacher cadre. If we could succeed in improving the work life of teachers in the less costly ways described previously, we would be able to retain a far higher proportion of younger teachers.

IN CONCLUSION

How can we briefly summarize the state of public education in the United States? We have seen that our students typically perform at a respectable level on international comparisons of student achievement. We've also seen that the 25 percent of students in our dysfunctional schools are depressing our overall student performance levels. More importantly, as a society we are squandering the potential talents and contributions of the 25 percent of our students who attend these shamefully deficient schools.

The condition of these schools is a critical national problem that has proven intractable, despite a steady stream of initiatives over more than forty-five years beginning with the passage of the Title I remedial program in 1965. The long-term survival of our society and form of government are in serious jeopardy because of the condition of public education in our most troubled communities.

On a more positive note, several improvements are attainable at a compara-tively low cost. These recommendations include greater parental involvement, high-stakes exit tests from secondary schools, and changing the distribution of vacation time over the course of the year. Other positive steps include a rigorous national curriculum, effective homework policies, and initiatives to improve the academic culture in schools.

The moderately costly suggestions include state or federal financing to improve beginning salaries for teachers early in their careers and raising the salaries of all teachers in our inner-city districts. These two initiatives regard-ing teacher salaries would cost $10 to $15 billion, or 2 percent of current expenditures in American schools. This investment would contribute greatly to attracting and retaining qualified teachers in all of our schools. To put this number in perspective, the federal Department of Education, which did not exist forty years ago, currently spends about $20 billion of its $71 billion budget each year for functions in addition to its funding of Title I, special education, and English-as-a-second-language programs.

Public schools in the United States are far better than the conventional wisdom of the pundit class would suggest. The steps suggested in this chap-ter, with the exception of those for improving our inner-city schools, do not require massive and expensive new programs nor the harnessing of national political energy or commitment to bring them about. Most of the improve-ments can be made at the local or state levels with little political controversy and modest financial commitment.

Parents have it within their power to increase the academic performance of their children and to promote and influence a greater level of academic emphasis in their own schools. It will be but a fairly short step to take our schools from good to great. The destiny of America's schools is ultimately in the hands of parents and local school communities.

Throughout this book many facts have been presented that suggest that there is much to admire in our public school system, along with serious problems that need to be addressed. Public schools provide a common bond to citizens in thousands of towns and urban neighborhoods across the country. They embody the ideal that every child should have an opportunity to become well educated. The public school experience also reinforces the concept that an increasingly diverse population can work together for the benefit of the general society.

Bibliography

American Institute for Economic Research. Cost of Living Calcuator. (n.d.). Retrieved March 4, 2010, from www.aier.org/research/worksheets-and-tools/cost-of-living-calculator.

Boe, E., and Shin, S. (2005). Is the United States really losing the international horse race in academic achievement? *Phi Delta Kappan 86*(9), 688–695.

Bolman, L., and Deal, T. (1991). *Reframing organizations: Artistry, choice and leadership.* San Francisco: Jossey-Bass.

Center for Union Facts. (2010). Teachers union facts. Retrieved February 16, 2010, from http://teachersunionexposed.com/protecting.cfm.

Chubb, J., and Moe, T. (1990). *Politics, markets and America's schools.* Washington, DC: Brookings Institution Press.

Covey, S. (1991). *The seven habits of highly effective people.* New York: Simon and Shuster.

Davidson, A. (2009, February 16). Country Day in Harlem. *Forbes.*

DiCarlo, M., Johnson, N., and Cochran, P. (2008). *Survey and analysis of teacher salary trends 2007.* Washington, DC: American Federation of Teachers.

Dillon, S. (2007, December 12). Report finds better scores in new crop of teachers. *New York Times.* Retrieved May 18, 2010, from www.nytimes.com/2007/12/12/education/12teachers.html?_r=1&scp=1&sq=%22drew+h.+gitomer%22&st=nyt.

Eckstein, M. A. (1994). *Great expectations: An international comparison of end-of-secondary school examinations.* Background paper prepared for a conference of the Office of Educational Research and Innovation. Washington, DC: Department of Education.

Fine, S. (2009, August 13). Why so many teachers get fed up. *The Week.* Retrieved May 26, 2010, from http://theweek.com/article/index/99567/why-so-many-teachers-get-fed-up.

Friedman, M. (1980). *Free to choose.* New York: Harcourt Brace Jovanovich.

Fullan, M. (1991). *The new meaning of educational change*, second ed. New York: New York Teachers College Press.

———. (2001). *Leading in a culture of change*. San Francisco: Jossey-Bass.

———. (2007). *The new meaning of educational change*, fourth ed. New York: New York Teachers College Press.

Gladwell, M. (2009). *What the dog saw.* New York: Little, Brown and Company.

Goodman, G. (2009). *School choice yearbook 2008–2009.* Washington, DC: Alliance for School Choice.

Grady, M., and Bryant, M. (1991). School board turmoil and superintendent turnover. *The School Administrator 29*: 68–72.

Grigg, W., and Dion, G. (2007). *The nation's report card: Mathematics 2007* (NCES 2007-494). National Center for Education Statistics, Institute of Education Sciences. Washington, DC: U.S. Department of Education.

Hafner, K. (2009, May 26). Texting may be taking a toll. *Wall Street Journal.* Retrieved June 26, 2010, from www.nytimes.com/2009/05/26/health/26teen.html.

Hechinger, J., and Dugan, I. J. (2009, September 22). Charter schools pass key test in study. *Wall Street Journal.* Retrieved May 19, 2010, from http://online.wsj.com/article/SB125358513141729871.html?KEYWORDS=%22charter+schools%22.

Hess, F. M. (2002). *School boards at the dawn of the 21st century.* Arlington, VA: National School Boards Association.

International Comparison of Productivity. (2008). United Kingdom: Office of National Statistics.

Lee, J., Grigg, W., and Donahue, P. (2007). *The nation's report card: Reading 2007* (NCES 2007-496). National Center for Education Statistics, Institute of Education Sciences. Washington, DC: U.S. Department of Education.

Marklein, M. B. (2009, June 3). 4-year colleges graduate 53% of students in 6 years. *USA Today.* Retrieved May 26, 2010, from www.usatoday.com/news/education/2009-06-03-diploma-graduation-rate_N.htm.

Martin, M. O., Mullis, I. V. S., Foy, P. in collaboration with Olson, J. F., Erberber, E., Preuschoff, C., and Galia, J. (2008). *TIMSS 2007 international science report: Findings from IEA's Trends in International Mathematics and Science Study at the fourth and eighth grades.* TIMSS and PIRLS International Study Center, Lynch School of Education. Boston: Boston College.

McAdams, R. (1972). *A study of the relationships between principal rated teaching effectiveness and the scholastic achievement of selected high school teachers of academic subjects.* Unpublished doctoral dissertation in education, Temple University.

———. (1993). *Lessons from abroad: How other countries educate their children.* Lancaster, PA: Technomic Publishing Company, Inc.

———. (1995). Interrelationships among property rate changes, school board member turnover, and superintendent turnover in selected Pennsylvania school districts. *Planning and Change 26*: 57–70.

———. (1997). A systems approach to school reform. *Phi Delta Kappan 79*(2): 138–142. Reprinted with permission of Phi Delta Kappa International, www.pdkintl.org. All rights reserved.

McQueen, M. P. (2010, February 12). Better education shields women from worst of job cuts. *Wall Street Journal*. Retrieved May 24, 2010, from http://online.wsj.com/article/SB10001424052748703389004575033762482114190.html?KEYWORDS=bachelor%27s+degree.

Mezzacappa, D. (2007, June 24). Pieces of an educational dream. Philly.com. Retrieved May 21, 2010, from www.philly.com/inquirer/education/2007The Belmont112TwentyYearsLater.html#axzz0obC6Mxq9.

Mullis, I. V. S., Martin, M. O., and Foy, P., in collaboration with Olson, J. F., Preuschoff, C., Erberber, E., Arora, A., and Galia, J. (2008). *TIMSS 2007 international mathematics report: Findings from IEA's Trends in International Mathematics and Science Study at the fourth and eighth grades.* TIMSS and PIRLS International Study Center, Lynch School of Education. Boston: Boston College.

Mullis, I. V. S., Martin, M. O., Kennedy, A. M., and Foy, P. (2007). *PIRLS 2006 international report.* TIMSS and PIRLS International Study Center, Lynch School of Education. Boston: Boston College.

National Commission on Excellence in Education. (1983). *A nation at risk: The imperative for educational reform.* Washington, DC: U.S. Department of Education.

National Institute of Mental Health. (2008). *The numbers count: Mental disorders in America, 2006.* Retrieved March 10, 2010, from www.nimh.nih.gov/health/publications/the-numbers-count-mental-disorders-in-america/index.shtml.

National Science Board. (2002). *Science and engineering indicators 2002* (volume 1, NSB 02-1). Arlington, VA: National Science Foundation.

———. (2004). *Science and engineering indicators. 2004* (volume 1, NSB 04-1; volume 2, NSB 04-1A). Arlington, VA: National Science Foundation.

No (tenured) teacher left behind. (2010, February 22). *Wall Street Journal*. Retrieved May 24, 2010, from http://online.wsj.com/article/SB10001424052748704804204575069502242529826.html.

Office of Innovation and Improvement. (2006). *Charter high schools: Closing the achievement gap.* Washington, DC: U.S. Department of Education.

Office of Management and Budget. (2010). *Budget of the U.S. government fiscal year 2011.* Washington, DC: Government Printing Office.

Organization for Economic Cooperation and Development. (2005). *Teachers matter: Attracting, developing and retaining effective teachers.* Paris: OECD Publishing.

———. (2008). *OECD Indicators.* Retrieved April 12, 2010, from www.oecd.org/edu/eag2008.

———. (2009). *Highlights from education at a glance.* Paris: OECD Publishing.

Parents Advocating School Accountability. (2009). Retrieved February 17, 2010, from www.pasasf.org/edison/edison.html.

Planty, M., Hussar, W., Snyder, T., Kena, G., KewalRamani, A., Kemp, J., Bianco, K., and Dinkes, R. (2009). *The condition of education 2009* (NCES 2009-081). National Center for Education Statistics, Institute of Education Sciences. Washington, DC: U.S. Department of Education.

Planty, M., Hussar, W., Snyder, T., Provasnik, S., Kena, G., Dinkes, R., KewalRamani, A., and Kemp, J. (2008). *The condition of education 2008* (NCES 2008-031).

National Center for Education Statistics, Institute of Education Sciences. Washington, DC: U.S. Department of Education.

Rampey, B. D., Dion, G. S., and Donahue, P. L. (2009). *NAEP 2008 trends in academic progress in reading and mathematics* (NCES 2009-479). National Center for Education Statistics, Institute of Education Sciences. Washington, DC: U.S. Department of Education.

Ravitch, Diane. (2010). *The death and life of the great American school system.* New York: Basic Books.

———. (2010, March 9). Why I changed my mind about school reform. *Wall Street Journal.* Retrieved May 24, 2010, from http://online.wsj.com/article/SB100014240 52748704869304575109443305343962.html?KEYWORDS=diane+ravitch.

Sarason, S. (1990). *The predictable failure of school reform.* San Francisco: Jossey-Bass.

Sawchuk, S. (2010, June 9). Merit-pay model pushed by Duncan shows no achievement edge. *Education Week 1:* 21.

Schlechty, P. (1990). *Schools for the 21st century.* San Francisco: Jossey-Bass.

Senge, P. (1990). *The fifth discipline.* New York: Doubleday.

Snyder, T. D., Dillow, S. A., and Hoffman, C. M. (2009). *Digest of education statistics 2008* (NCES 2009-020). National Center for Education Statistics, Institute of Education Sciences. Washington, DC: U.S. Department of Education.

Southeast Regional Vision for Education. (1994). *Overcoming barriers to school reform.* Washington, DC: U.S. Department of Education.

Stollsteimer, J. (2010, June 16). Give us the truth about school violence. *Education Week 29*(35): 34.

"Third of boys fail to graduate, study finds." (2006, April 20). *Washington Times.* Retrieved May 24, 2010, from www.washingtontimes.com/news/2006/apr/20/20060420-110857-3996r/.

Tough, Paul. (2004, June 20). The Harlem project. *New York Times.* Retrieved May 26, 2010, from www.nytimes.com/2004/06/20/magazine/the-harlem-project .html?sec=health.

U.S. Department of Commerce, Bureau of the Census. (2007). *Summary of local government finances—School systems 2007.* Washington DC: Government Printing Office.

U.S. Department of Education. (2010). Fiscal year 2010 budget summary. Retrieved March 16, 2010, from www2.ed.gov/about/overview/budget/budget10/summary/ edlite-section1.html.

Woodall, M. (2009, October 23). Ex-charter school chief sentenced to 3 years. *Philadelphia Inquirer*, A01.

Woodall, M., and Shiffman, J. (2009, August 16). Off the charts: Charter school probes expand. *Philadelphia Inquirer*, B01.

About the Author

Richard McAdams began his career as a science teacher from 1965 to 1969. His first administrative position was as a junior high principal. He next served as principal of a seventeen-hundred-student high school in suburban Philadelphia. He attained his first superintendent's position in 1976, serving for fifteen years in the same district. He taught graduate educational leadership courses as an assistant professor at Lehigh University from 1994 to 2000. While at Lehigh, he served as executive director of the Lehigh University School Study Council—a professional development consortium of forty school district superintendents. In recent years he has served as an interim superintendent in two school districts. He is the author of two previous books on educational topics, *Lessons from Abroad: How Other Countries Educate Their Children* and *Performance Appraisal of School Management.* He received his doctoral degree from Temple University.